Especially for

....

From

....

Date

....

Anita Higman & Marian Leslie

How God Grows *a* Woman of Faith

BARBOUR BOOKS

An Imprint of Barbour Publishing, Inc.

Published by Barbour Books, an imprint of Barbour Publishing, Inc., 1810 Barbour Drive, Uhrichsville, Ohio 44683, www.barbourbooks.com

Our mission is to inspire the world with the life-changing message of the Bible.

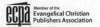

Member of the
Evangelical Christian
Publishers Association

To Janice Thompson:

Thank you for being
such a beloved friend.
You inspire me
with your courage,
your Christlike love,
and your generosity of heart!
–Anita Higman

To Joanna and Wendy:

My faithful and faith-filled friends.
–Marian Leslie

Introduction

Having faith in God seems like such a doable spiritual goal—until our dreams begin to crumble. Suddenly faith can become no more than a flighty feeling. In those dark nights of trouble, faith might even appear to be spiritual wishful thinking—an achievement to be pursued only in the mind, but never realized.

But with the Lord ever by our side, all that we need for this life adventure is before us. All the encouragement. All the supernatural power. All the love. Everything we need to take steps—no matter how rocky or narrow the path—has been provided. God will even strengthen our faith when we ask. Just as one ancient follower exclaimed, "I believe, Lord. Help my unbelief!"—may that honest cry to our Abba Father ever be on our hearts.

Come with us now as we explore together this wonderfully daring and miraculous journey of the soul.

Faith.

Hello, God. . . It's Me

*Now faith is confidence in what we hope for
and assurance about what we do not see.*
HEBREWS 11:1

Do you ever hear yourself saying something like, "Hello, God, it's me again. I'm such a mess right now; You may want to look away from me."

We've all arrived before God with different levels of faith. There is the stalwart faith that marches out of the pages of an old hymnal. Then there are weary days, depressed days. And some days you wonder if even a mustard seed of faith would be impossible.

God allows us to come before Him just as we are. We may think we have too many hopes for Him to handle. We may think we haven't seen a miracle in so long that we're not sure God is listening, let alone willing to meet our needs. But no matter where we are in our faith journey, our Lord says, "Come."

And as we come before Him we may ask for more faith—just as a follower exclaimed in the book of Mark, "I do believe; help me overcome my unbelief!" (Mark 9:24).

*Oh, merciful God, thank You for loving me even
on days when my faith is slim. Please bring me once
again to a place of trust in You. Amen. —A.H.*

When Your Smile Cannot Be Found

May the God of hope fill you with all joy and
peace as you trust in him, so that you may overflow
with hope by the power of the Holy Spirit.
ROMANS 15:13

Do you sometimes gaze into the mirror and wonder where your smile went off to? Like maybe it headed out to a sunny beach, where sailboats dip and sway in a crystal blue sea? Well, you *can* get your smile back!

Romans 15:13 reminds us that if we trust in the Lord, then peace and joy will be ours. The more we hand over our daily burdens to the One who can truly handle them, then the more we can be free to enjoy our lives and do all that God created us to do. We can breathe again, and our aching spirits can find refreshment. We can move forward with more creativity, more passion, more energy, more laughter.

You *can* get your smile back. It all comes down to trusting in the One who is and always desires to be faithfully yours.

Lord, please allow Your Holy Spirit to strengthen my
trust in You—that I can find joy and peace in this life, and
that these blessings will overflow onto others, bringing
them hope. In Jesus' name I pray. Amen. —A.H.

Out of the Boat

"Lord, if it's you," Peter replied, "tell me to come to you on the water." "Come," he said. Then Peter got down out of the boat, walked on the water and came toward Jesus.

MATTHEW 14:28–29

Have you ever asked yourself, "Who am I when it comes to faith in God?" What do we do when times get rough? Maybe not physically rough, like the seas described by Matthew, but what happens when we experience storms of the soul? Do we walk onward with courage, without doubting the Lord's ability to guide us through? Do we take Jesus' challenge to come and trust Him? Or are we like the other men in the boat? Do we hang back and wait for other believers to charge forth, especially when risk is involved?

Are we more like the Peter who got right out of the boat, or are we more like the Peter who faltered?

If you are more like Peter when he fell to pieces, ask the Holy Spirit to bolster your faith—to remind you of the times when He rescued you. To remind you of the Lord who walks on the stormy sea and reaches out, saying "Come."

Lord Jesus, please help me to remember the miracles of the past, the many times You came to my rescue. May I use those memories to increase my faith in the future. Amen. —A.H.

Darkness You Can Feel

Then the LORD said to Moses, "Stretch out your hand toward the sky so that darkness spreads over Egypt—darkness that can be felt."
EXODUS 10:21

Have you ever been in a show cave when the tour guide switches off all the lights for a few moments? They pull this startling stunt on tourists so people can experience total darkness. Usually there are a few chuckles and humorous comments, but after a few seconds—like the Egyptians of old in Exodus—visitors are anxiously awaiting the return of the light.

True darkness is so penetrating one can almost feel it. The tour guides will tell you that the cave's deepest darkness will, after a month, cause blindness and then later, insanity. To contemplate complete spiritual darkness is enough to make one shudder. Many would say that our world is in the midst of a plague of darkness and depravity, which means that we should flee from sin—from anything that is contrary to the Lord's teachings—and into the Light of the world, Jesus Christ. You will feel Christ's radiant and holy light all the way to your soul.

So, take heart! Keep the faith. There need not be any more spiritual darkness as you allow Christ to become the light of your life!

Lord, thank You for bringing Your light into this dark and hurting world! Amen. —A.H.

To Higher Ground

Then he said to Thomas, "Put your finger here; see my hands. Reach out your hand and put it into my side. Stop doubting and believe." Thomas said to him, "My Lord and my God!" Then Jesus told him, "Because you have seen me, you have believed; blessed are those who have not seen and yet have believed."
JOHN 20:27–29

That word—*doubt*—is enough to start a slow trickle of sweat down our spines. We know that word too intimately, and it affects every part of our lives.

When Jesus appeared to the disciples after His resurrection, Thomas doubted it was Him until he saw the scars. How would we react? Would we be the doubter, or the one who believed Jesus had fulfilled all He'd promised?

For Christians, doubting can either debilitate us spiritually or bring us to higher ground. Remembering all the many ways that the Lord has come to our rescue time and time again through the years is one way to find that higher ground. It is human to doubt. But the Lord asks us to believe Him. In fact, He told Thomas, "Because you have seen me, you have believed; blessed are those who have not seen and yet have believed." May the Lord find us faithful. Jesus says these followers will be raised up and filled with joy. May it be so!

Lord, may my faith in You grow ever stronger in the days and years to come. Amen. —A.H.

In Good Company

*Then the word of the LORD came to him: "This man will not be
your heir, but a son who is your own flesh and blood will be your
heir." He took him outside and said, "Look up at the sky and
count the stars—if indeed you can count them." Then he said
to him, "So shall your offspring be." Abram believed the
LORD, and he credited it to him as righteousness.*

GENESIS 15:4–6

Admit it, when you think of some of the distinguished characters
from the Old Testament like Abraham and Moses and David, it's
easy to say, "There is no way I can ever be as noble as those ancient
Bible heroes. I might as well give up now." And yet, as stalwart and
righteous as these leaders were at times, they too had severe bouts
of humanness as they stumbled in their walks with the Almighty.
Read some of those Bible passages surrounding their lives, and you
will see how true that statement really is. You are in good company.

Romans 3:23 tells us, "For all have sinned and fall short of the
glory of God." Yes, even though Abraham's life wasn't perfect, his
faith in God was looked upon as righteousness. We too can become
renowned people—great women—of virtue. We can make the choice
to trust God in all His promises. It's a decision Abraham made, and
it's a daily choice we can make too!

May I trust in You, Lord, every day, every hour. Amen. —A.H.

Don't Get Too Comfortable

My Father's house has many rooms; if that were not so,
would I have told you that I am going there to prepare a place
for you? And if I go and prepare a place for you, I will come back
and take you to be with me that you also may be where I am.
You know the way to the place where I am going.
JOHN 14:2–4

There's sad news. And there's incredible news. The sad news is we're all going to die. The incredible news is that Jesus has conquered death on the cross, and we can have life eternal with Him. Yes, as followers of Christ, we are just passing through this dusty, war-torn, sin-stained, sorrow-laden land, and moving on to our celestial homeland—heaven.

Just imagine. Hope fully realized. Radiance beyond the sun. Laughter like a song. Friendships that have no conditions. Love with no end. Beauty. Goodness. Joy. Splendor. Gifts of knowledge and understanding and creative genius that we cannot even fathom. And best of all, walking with God!

Yes, let's not get too comfortable here. Why would we want to? Jesus is preparing a place, and He will someday take us home so we can be with Him forever. Jesus has transformed death into life, darkness into light, and an ending into a miraculous new beginning!

Thank You, Lord, for the promise of heaven. Amen. —A.H.

Live Life Fully!

"Therefore I tell you, do not worry about your life, what you will eat or drink; or about your body, what you will wear. Is not life more than food, and the body more than clothes? Look at the birds of the air; they do not sow or reap or store away in barns, and yet your heavenly Father feeds them. Are you not much more valuable than they? Can any one of you by worrying add a single hour to your life?"
MATTHEW 6:25–27

Are you an authority on worry? You could create a useful study guide on the topic. Maybe you could even teach at the college level!

Worry is a spiritual malady we have all suffered from, and yet Jesus doesn't want us to fret. He wants us to take His hand and run far away from the taunting lies of the enemy. He wants to lead us to a place of peace, where we can know His hope and live in His victory. Where we can trust Him with our troubles so very well that we can see the rainbows in a dewdrop again, chase fireflies in the dusk, and pick bouquets of wildflowers just to bring someone a smile. He wants us to enjoy life. To love and be loved. And how can that happen when our lives are strangled with worry?

*Lord, may I trust You greatly that
I might live life fully! Amen. —A.H.*

A Faith-Leap of the Heart

For we live by faith, not by sight.
2 Corinthians 5:7

People aren't comfortable with the concept of faith in God, because it involves our hearts and not just our heads. And that scares us.

But God says, "We live by faith, not by sight." That's not exactly the world's way of doing things. Yet daily we have to exercise faith in every area of our lives.

Even though God is veiled to us right now—He has given us His holy Word as a testimony, His Son, Jesus, as a sacrifice, and the Holy Spirit as a comforter and teacher. In spite of various objections to having faith in an unseen Creator God, He has proved throughout the ages to be steadfast and just and loving. He is worthy of a most serious faith-leap!

Have you held your heart back out of doubt or fears or concern over what your family, friends, and coworkers might say? Taking that soul-dive is indeed life altering, and it has beautiful ramifications not only for the present but throughout eternity.

Lord, I take that plunge into Your mercy, grace, forgiveness, and freedom. Please teach me how to live by faith in You and not by sight. Amen. —A.H.

The Art of Rescue

*Do not be anxious about anything, but in
every situation, by prayer and petition,
with thanksgiving, present your requests to God.*

PHILIPPIANS 4:6

We've all had fussy-fretting days. If we had a bird's-eye view of humans during those episodes, we might look like a writhing pile of ants after the mound had been given a good, healthy stomp.

But we can all relate to matters of worry. Worrying can and does get the best of us sometimes. Hard for it not to when we're bombarded with every kind of trauma—bad news at the doctor's office, car accidents, rebellious teenagers, job loss, bankruptcy, misunderstandings, depression, pay cuts, death of loved ones, failed businesses, betrayals, consequences of sinful choices, disappointments, divorce, and loneliness, just to name a few. After looking through that list it's a wonder we humans can make it through a month, let alone a lifetime of troubles!

But we serve a God who throughout the ages has come to the rescue of humankind—from great nations down to a single, hurting soul. He was there. And He is here now. We serve the same God who held nothing back—not even His own Son.

Instead of worry, may we always approach our Lord with requests and thanksgiving. In a world drowning in a sea of sufferings, our Lord is the master of the art of rescue!

*I renounce worry, Lord, and I will instead place all
my requests into Your capable hands. Amen. —A.H.*

Have You Noticed?

All Scripture is inspired by God and is useful to teach us what is true and to make us realize what is wrong in our lives. It corrects us when we are wrong and teaches us to do what is right.
2 Timothy 3:16 NLT

Do you believe the Bible?

Have you noticed that what used to be considered the essentials of the Christian faith are slowly evolving or disintegrating all together? Fewer and fewer people view the Bible as the inspired Word of God. A growing number of people believe that the Bible is just a fascinating storybook.

Perhaps this belittling of God's holy Word stems from wanting to be politically correct or from pursuing our own desires, rather than following the wise precepts of the Lord—teachings that keep us from going astray spiritually.

Perhaps this "falling away" from the Word of God is the reason for our society's decline into the plagues of corruption, depravity, and violence. Matthew 12:30 (MSG) says, "This is war, and there is no neutral ground. If you're not on my side, you're the enemy; if you're not helping, you're making things worse."

So, in this spiritual war we live in—it would be good to ask ourselves—whose side are we truly on?

Lord Jesus, I believe the Bible to be the inspired Word of God, and I want to follow You all the days of my life. Amen. —A.H.

A Servant's Heart

"For even the Son of Man did not come to be served,
but to serve, and to give his life as a ransom for many."
MARK 10:45

We might secretly think that having a servant's heart is a tedious, wasteful, lowly, noncreative, unrewarding, unglamorous, and messy way to live. Not to mention unappreciated!

And yet that is exactly what Jesus did. He came not just as the King of kings and the Lord of lords, but to be a servant and to give Himself up as a living sacrifice for us. What unfathomable dedication and love!

When you do reach out in faith and choose to serve in the ways God has called you to, things begin to happen. Powerful things. You may find you have more time on your hands than you thought you would. You might feel more peace and love and joy trickling into your spirit than you ever imagined.

Serving others can mean a thousand different things. Open your heart to a servant's mind-set. Ask God about it. He'll show you just what you were created to do. And then—well, expect joy!

Lord, please give me the willingness, enthusiasm,
and energy to serve others. I want to please
You in every part of my life. Amen. —A.H.

Do You Love Me?

*The third time he said to him, "Simon son of John, do you love
me?" Peter was hurt because Jesus asked him the third time,
"Do you love me?" He said, "Lord, you know all things;
you know that I love you." Jesus said, "Feed my sheep."*
JOHN 21:17

When you love your child—really love your child—you always hope
and dream that they will love you back. It's part of what makes a
beautiful family relationship.

God loves His children deeply, and He too hopes we will love
Him right back and help create that beautiful family relationship.
How do we know of God's love? The Bible is full of references
to His divine love. And He sent Jesus, His Son, to walk among
us and to make a way for our broken relationship to be mended
with our Father in heaven.

In John 21:17, Jesus asks Peter three times if he does indeed
love Him. Even though there may be a number of reasons Jesus
asked this question the way He did, no doubt our Lord hoped for
that loving response. Christianity isn't just a religion—it's a relationship between the Creator of the universe and His beloved. It's that
simple, that profound, that real.

Have you answered Jesus' question yet? "Do you love Me?"

*Oh, Lord, may I always respect You as my Creator
God but also love You as a daughter would
love her beloved Father. Amen. —A.H.*

If You Could Distill Your Life

*But the fruit of the Spirit is love, joy, peace, forbearance,
kindness, goodness, faithfulness, gentleness and self-control.
Against such things there is no law.*

GALATIANS 5:22–23

If you could distill your life down to a handful of words, what would they be? Or—to take this game to a scarier level—what would your family, friends, and coworkers say if they could summarize your life? *Oh dear.* Would they think of you as loving? Joyful? Peaceful? Disciplined? Patient? Kind? Good? Faithful? Gentle? In other words, does your life have the sweet aroma of the mature and mellow fruits of the Spirit that are listed in Galatians 5:22–23? Or would others think your spirit smelled a bit more like rotten fruit?!

If you have failed in producing these good fruits (and we *all* have failed on occasion), there is hope. There is time to make some changes. Time to grow. Time to turn our hearts toward heaven. And the Lord will be glad to help you. You only need to ask!

*Lord, I need some serious help with my spirit. I want to
become more like You every day, but I can't do any of this alone.
Please help me to be filled with love, joy, peace, forbearance,
kindness, goodness, faithfulness, gentleness, and self-control!
In Jesus' name I pray. Amen. —A.H.*

In All Your Ways

Trust in and rely confidently on the Lord with all your heart and do not rely on your own insight or understanding. In all your ways know and acknowledge and recognize Him, And He will make your paths straight and smooth [removing obstacles that block your way].

PROVERBS 3:5–6 AMP

Trust in the Lord? Yes, it sounds like something good to add to our ongoing spiritual list of stuff to improve our Christian journey. So we'll begin with Proverbs 3:5–6.

Uh-oh, you might be thinking. You mean I'm supposed to trust the Lord completely, and I'm *not* to rely on my own insights? Hmm. Got to think about that one.

Our insights in this life are very limited. We cannot know all things as God does. Only the Lord can redeem our past, guide us through the present, and help us plan for the future.

When we demand to do life our way—that is, with more faith in our own abilities than in God's—we find that our paths grow crooked. But if we know the Lord, acknowledge Him, and recognize Him, He will make our paths straight!

Lord Jesus, help me to let go of my own flawed ways and look to You for guidance in all areas of my life. Amen. —A.H.

Mourning into Dancing!

In their fright the women bowed down with their faces to the ground, but the men said to them, "Why do you look for the living among the dead? He is not here; he has risen! Remember how he told you, while he was still with you in Galilee."

LUKE 24:5–6

Everything changed that one Easter morning. That one moment when the tomb no longer symbolized death, but life. But Jesus' followers seemed surprised over the unoccupied burial chamber. So much so, that the angels asked them, "Why do you look for the living among the dead?" Had Jesus' followers forgotten His words or lacked in faith?

Soon shock would turn into understanding, and they would never ever be the same. Yes, surely they thought "nothing" never looked so good. "Empty" never glowed with such promise. And "quiet" never held so much rejoicing!

Everything we do and say and believe as Christians rests on that one empty tomb. It changes the course of history, and it changes one heart at a time. We can be forever grateful for Easter morning. The miracle that turned night into day, shadow into radiance, and mourning into dancing!

So, take courage. His promises are fulfilled. Redemption is ours. Love wins. Hallelujah!

Thank You, Lord, for loving us enough to give us that Easter morning. Amen. —A.H.

A Raging Battle

*In every battle you will need faith as your shield
to stop the fiery arrows aimed at you by Satan.*
EPHESIANS 6:16 TLB

When chatting over coffee, it's uncommon for people to converse about the supernatural world. It's just not considered an easy or safe subject for conversation.

But when you pin people down on the topic, many do not believe in the supernatural world—and yet according to the Word of God, it is a very real realm. In fact, there is a battle raging for your soul. Satan is determined to find your greatest weaknesses and he will start firing at you until he has you where he wants you. Lost. Lonely. Stumbling without hope. And sick in body, mind, and spirit.

But faith is like a shield against those dark attacks. A trusting commitment to the Lord—that we believe in Him, love Him, and serve Him—gives us the supernatural power to come against the most powerful, fiery arrows from Satan. We need not fear the enemy of our souls. We only need to be strong in our faith in the Lord.

*Lord Jesus, show me how not to waver in my faith,
but to be ever strong, so that I may stand against
the enemy of my soul. Amen. —A.H.*

A Love like That

No, in all these things we are more than conquerors through him who loved us. For I am convinced that neither death nor life, neither angels nor demons, neither the present nor the future, nor any powers, neither height nor depth, nor anything else in all creation, will be able to separate us from the love of God that is in Christ Jesus our Lord.

ROMANS 8:37–39

Have you ever loved someone so much—truly adored someone so deeply—that when the slightest tension arose between the two of you—well, you couldn't wait another hour, not even another moment, to make it right? You wanted all to be well so you could make the relationship just the way it was? So you could run into his arms with abandon?

Yes, we have the ability to love in such a glorious and generous way, and yet our Father in heaven loves us even more deeply, more lavishly, more fervently.

Let us always want to make things right with our Lord as quickly as possible. Let us run into His welcoming arms. Let us love Christ—without fear, without reservation. So much so that the world looks on and says, "I too want a love like that!"

Lord, thank You for Your great love. Please show me how to love You more deeply every day. Amen. —A.H.

Praying without Believing

When she recognized Peter's voice, she was so overjoyed she ran back without opening it and exclaimed, "Peter is at the door!" "You're out of your mind," they told her. When she kept insisting that it was so, they said, "It must be his angel." But Peter kept on knocking, and when they opened the door and saw him, they were astonished.

ACTS 12:14–16

This passage from Acts hits a bit too close to home, doesn't it? A gathering of believers had been praying for Peter's release from prison, but when the prayer was answered and Peter did indeed show up at the door, the prayer warriors didn't believe the news. They thought the man was surely an angel, rather than Peter!

When we pray, are we just going through the motions, or do we really expect a miracle? For instance, when we pray fervently for relief from a drought, do we believe the sky will open up with showers from heaven, or do we head out on our errands without even the thought of taking a raincoat?

Do our actions speak louder than our prayers?

Lord, when I come to You, help me to believe in Your faithfulness to hear me and answer my prayer! Amen. —A.H.

Never Ready for the Ragbag

"For I know the plans I have for you," declares the Lord,
"plans to prosper you and not to harm you,
plans to give you hope and a future."
Jeremiah 29:11

A ragbag is a bag where you keep old rags. Sounds like a sad little place, doesn't it? Sometimes we get the idea we've been designated to an old ragbag—a place where you toss things that have nearly been used up.

We go along with the idea that we are too tired, too ill, or too old to accomplish what we're called to do. Or maybe we believe we're lacking the right background, education, social skills, money, or platform to fulfill our purpose.

Then again, maybe we're just thinking of the wrong purpose. God has something in mind for us that may be far beyond what we can imagine.

Bottom line—if you wake up for another day on this side of eternity, then the Lord has a plan for you to be here. It may not necessarily be something from one of your lists, but make no mistake, it'll be on His. We should let go of the world's thinking, and go with the way of God!

Lord, show me the reason I am here, both for now
and all the days You've given me. Amen. —A.H.

Mercy

Oh, give thanks to the God of heaven!
For His mercy endures forever.
PSALM 136:26 NKJV

What if, for reasons of careless and immoral behavior, you somehow built up a huge financial liability—an unpayable debt so serious that it put you in prison? Then what if a friend, one who was known for his mercy, cut a check, paying your debt in full? What a compassionate deed, to set you free from that dark and dank place!

You can now watch those rusty gates swing open. You can step outside into the warm sunshine and smell the sweet fragrant day. What would you do? You might laugh with astonishment at such an undeserved gift. You might weep a while too, in gratitude to be out of the frightful place you were in. And thank the one who set you free.

Our Lord Jesus paid a similar debt for our sinful ways. He set us free from an awful place of darkness. He paid the debt not with money but with His very life. All we have to do is accept the mercy, the grace, and the love.

But wouldn't a big "thank you" be lovely?

Lord, I thank You for this great and unfathomable gift of mercy, when You paid my debt of sin on the cross. Amen. —A.H.

Such a Tiny Thing

He replied, "Because you have so little faith. Truly I tell you,
if you have faith as small as a mustard seed, you can say to
this mountain, 'Move from here to there,' and it will move.
Nothing will be impossible for you."
MATTHEW 17:20

People love living large. And we like supersized stuff. *Mega*, *ultra*, and *whopper* are popular words of the day. But when it comes to faith in God, sometimes huge doesn't always come up. We can at times be people of smallish faith. Maybe Jesus gave us the image of the mustard seed so we wouldn't get too discouraged when we want to believe big but our flesh gets in the way.

If you've never seen a mustard seed, these tiny pearls are very small, only three millimeters in diameter. But they do grow into trees large enough to support birds nesting in their branches. Amazing that something so minuscule has such potential. And that is how we can be encouraged!

When you think that your faith is smallish, remember Jesus' words about the mustard seed and be reassured and raised in spirit. With God's help, our simple, rather unimpressive faith can bring about a miracle of mammoth proportion. We should be expectant, joyful, and inspired!

Lord, please take my mustard seed of faith and
make it grow into something wonderful! Amen. —A.H.

All My Forevers

We are confident, I say, and would prefer to be
away from the body and at home with the Lord.
2 CORINTHIANS 5:8

When a man and a woman fall in love and get engaged, they usually do their best to get to know each other better before they're married. The woman might discover her fiancé's favorite man-cave hobby, and he might find out which ice cream brings his fiancée the merriest grin. They will memorize what causes each other pain, laughter, sadness, or joy—the best ways to please and delight each other.

As Christians, wouldn't we too want to know the many wonderful facets of God? We aren't marrying the Lord, but what we have with Him is a real relationship, and we won't just be spending fifty golden years with Him, but all eternity! Wouldn't we want to know the thoughts and behaviors that would disappoint, grieve, or anger the Lord? What words and deeds might bring Him delight?

Reading God's Word and praying to Him are two ways to discover His attributes and the many ways to get to know Him more intimately and to fall in love with Him more deeply.

I am looking forward to getting to know You better,
Lord. And I'm looking forward to spending all
my forevers with You! Amen. —A.H.

Misplaced Anger

This righteousness is given through faith in Jesus Christ to all who believe. There is no difference between Jew and Gentile, for all have sinned and fall short of the glory of God, and all are justified freely by his grace through the redemption that came by Christ Jesus.

ROMANS 3:22–24

At times we do things that must grieve the Holy Spirit, as well as baffle the angels. Say your cousin Matilda apologizes for deliberately offending you, but later she gets angry at herself. *And* angry with you. You may wonder how that can be. After all, the woman's guilt reeks like rotten mackerel! Unfortunately, this backlash of remorse is pretty universal.

The offending party—never us, of course!—might make a genuine apology, but then other emotions tend to slither their way in. Somewhere in the process, people become masters at denial, defense, and deflection.

So wouldn't it be better for us to err on the side of humility (that is, to apologize and mean it), rather than to deny all wrongdoing and potentially continue in sin? The answer is clear, the grace is free, and God's redemption is real!

Lord, I have sinned against Your beloved.
But I have faith that You will forgive me. Amen. —A.H.

God's Circle of Love

*My brothers and sisters, believers in our glorious
Lord Jesus Christ must not show favoritism.*
JAMES 2:1

Even as adults, sometimes we play childish social games. We may even choose to exclude people from our lives for various reasons. Do we think of them as lacking in social skills or education? Do they seem too depressed, too gangly, or too overweight? Maybe another is disabled in some way or so poor and disheveled it makes us uncomfortable. So we choose to leave that person out of the conversation, out of our lives and our circle. Or even deny someone a friendly smile. Have you ever been the one left out? It's definitely not a cloud-nine experience!

But oh, isn't it marvelous that we worship a God who doesn't play favorites? His heart is big enough for everyone. Jesus didn't come to create private clubs or exclusive societies to keep people out. He instead offers His love, mercy, and grace to everyone. Christ invites all who will come into the kingdom of God. That is just like His love. It's the kind of openhearted love He hopes we will extend to others.

*I am so grateful, God, that You offer Your circle of love
to everyone. You are worthy of my devotion, my worship,
and my faith! In Jesus' name I pray. Amen. —A.H.*

Do You See Me, God?

She gave this name to the LORD who spoke to her:
"You are the God who sees me," for she said,
"I have now seen the One who sees me."
GENESIS 16:13

Older people sometimes feel left out of life, almost invisible to the rest of the world. And perhaps younger people feel they are not truly "seen" if they are deficient in what the world deems important.

But unlike humankind's fickle and fiendish ways, God *sees* you in all your glory, no matter your age. No matter what. He's known you since the first day you were knit in the womb, and He's loved you every day since then!

In Genesis we read of a woman in ancient times who felt unseen. Hagar, Sarah's handmaid, was mistreated and fled to the desert. Pregnant and scared, she must have felt so alone. But an angel of God reassured her and promised that God would bless her with many descendants. Then Hagar realized that God was with her. He saw her. And no matter what came next, she could return to her mistress, because God would be with her still.

When you think you are unseen by the world—for whatever reason—take comfort in the fact that God *sees* you and He cares for you deeply. He is faithful!

Thank You, Lord, for seeing me and
caring for me! Amen. —A.H.

I Need Serious Help!

In view of all this, make every effort to respond to God's promises. Supplement your faith with a generous provision of moral excellence, and moral excellence with knowledge.

2 PETER 1:5 NLT

God's Word advises us to have a generous amount of moral excellence as well as knowledge. *Hmm*, you might think, *I honestly don't think I can jump any higher or be any finer. I'm just me, and on more days than I'd like to admit, "me" is just not good enough.*

You're going to need some serious supernatural help. Doesn't everybody? Well, God is able and He's willing. He loves an honest heart, and a heart that is seeking a closer walk with Him.

When you read God's Word, ask the Holy Spirit for discernment and wisdom that you might grow daily in your knowledge of Him. As you make decisions throughout the day, ask the Lord for guidance, that you will please Him with choices of moral excellence. And then trust fully in His power that He can do all things. These are the ways to world-proof your life. These are the ways of heaven and joy!

Help me, Lord, to respond to Your promises. Please add moral excellence and knowledge to my faith in You. Amen. —A.H.

I'm Dining with the King

If we confess our sins, he is faithful and just and will forgive us our sins and purify us from all unrighteousness.

1 JOHN 1:9

Repentance and forgiveness are beautiful things. They make for truly miraculous moments when we are washed clean of our sins and made fresh and fragrant and beautiful. It's as if the Lord dresses us like a new bride, standing just so in our finery. Praise God! Let us go forth and celebrate with Him!

But sometimes we refuse to forgive ourselves and we refuse to celebrate. We listen to old messages that play in our heads—of unworthiness or whatever lies Satan can throw at us. But we have a choice. We can either accept this summons from the enemy to wallow in his mudhole, or we can accept an invitation to dine at the head table with the King of kings.

Would you really want to sully your pristine gown in a pigsty-like pool of filth? God is faithful. If we confess our sins, He will forgive us and purify us from all unrighteousness.

May we always choose the invitation from the King!

Thank You, Lord Jesus, that You are faithful to forgive me for my sins. We have much to celebrate! Amen. —A.H.

They Are Beloved

*But I say to you, love your enemies, bless those who
curse you, do good to those who hate you, and pray
for those who spitefully use you and persecute you.*

MATTHEW 5:44 NKJV

Most of us don't have many true enemies. But we may have a lot
of frenemies. You know, a coworker who makes you want to duck
into a supply closet to avoid chitchat. You can be a vibrant Christian
woman who's come a long way in her faith until *she* shows up,
and then you're reduced to a baby believer blubbering in the corner.
Truth be told, you have a secret name for *her*, but not a name
you could use at any church gatherings.

But God knows the name you use. In fact, He knows every one
of those people you dislike, or maybe even hate. He knows their
names and He loves each one of them. They are beloved in His sight.

We need to love the unlovable. Befriend the frenemies. Because
the more we pray for those who mistreat us, the more we crowd
out the ugly thoughts against them and the desires for retaliation.
God is holy, and He can be trusted to do what is just and good.
Do we trust Him with everything?

*Please show me how to see my enemies
through Your eyes, Lord. Amen. —A.H.*

Redemptive Power!

*And so, dear brothers, now we may walk right into the very
Holy of Holies, where God is, because of the blood of Jesus.
This is the fresh, new, life-giving way that Christ has opened
up for us by tearing the curtain—his human body—
to let us into the holy presence of God.*

HEBREWS 10:19–20 TLB

Mice run away, yes, but not without making a few women release a symphony of bloodcurdling screams. Mice scurrying back to the safety of their holes might remind you of how some Christians cower, almost as if embarrassed by the Gospel. And yet, aren't we to be bold in our faith? Yes, the Bible does say blessed are those who are meek, but that term refers to being teachable and humble and honorable. It's not referring to the boldness we can know in Christ.

As Christians we have every reason to reach out to a hurting world with confidence in what Christ can do through us.

May we then approach all those who need us not with an attitude of judgment but one of winsomeness and truth and love. If we have the right to walk into the holy of holies where God is because of the blood of Christ, we can also valiantly tell people of the good news of His redemptive power!

*Holy Spirit, show me how to be bold in sharing
the good news of the Gospel! Amen. —A.H.*

That Dusty Road

Take my yoke upon you. Let me teach you, because I am humble and gentle at heart, and you will find rest for your souls. For my yoke is easy to bear, and the burden I give you is light.
MATTHEW 11:29–30 NLT

You walk a dusty road and you feel that familiar load—whatever the name of it might be. You have been dragging that shabby old bag around your whole life. From the moment you wake up in the morning to the minute you go to sleep, that bulky, ugly thing is right by your side. Even your dreams are riddled with the oppression of those emotional belongings.

But that is not the way of God.

In a world with issues beyond anything we can bear, Jesus said these comforting words from Matthew 11 to us—and to you (v. 28 NLT): "Come to me, all of you who are weary and carry heavy burdens, and I will give you rest." He promises rest for your soul. He offers to refresh you with His teaching, and to trade your heavy burdens for His light one.

How wonderful to love and serve a God who makes such an offer. Have you chosen the way of God?

Oh, how I thank You, Lord Jesus, for Your faithful and gentle promises. Amen. —A.H.

The Way of Love

Love does not delight in evil but rejoices with the truth. It always protects, always trusts, always hopes, always perseveres.
1 CORINTHIANS 13:6–7

To love—truly love with one's whole being—is not so easy these days. That is, in an age of evil and danger and mistrust. It's almost as if our world is so full of hate, as if we are narrowing our eyes so much at every word and deed, that we have forgotten the ways of love. God's way.

Reading 1 Corinthians 13—the love chapter of the Bible—is an enlightening experience, inspiring us to undergo some serious beauty treatments for the soul.

In 1 Corinthians 13:4–5 we learn that "Love is patient, love is kind. It does not envy, it does not boast, it is not proud. It does not dishonor others, it is not self-seeking, it is not easily angered, it keeps no record of wrongs."

Such heaven-sent precepts! These are words that our sinful world has misplaced and it's a lifestyle we've forgotten. May God help us to find the words again—find the love and live it.

Holy Spirit, show me the way of true love for You, for my family, and for all humankind. Amen. —A.H.

One Glorious Day!

For it is by grace you have been saved, through faith—
and this is not from yourselves, it is the gift of God—
not by works, so that no one can boast.

EPHESIANS 2:8–9

You finally can afford a housekeeper for one glorious day, but suddenly you panic. You break out in a cold sweat as you think, *Oh no, she'll see my mess. She'll see all that old junk piled high in my closets. She might even get the idea that I'm—gasp—a hoarder! Maybe I need to clean things a bit. Tidy up. And if that isn't enough, I'll hide the rest!*

Isn't that just what we do when we think of God's grace? He wants us to come to Him just the way we are. Right now—this minute, in the middle of our sin. Not after we've tried and tried and tried to clean up our spiritual acts. We can't. We never could.

That's why it's called grace.

Unmerited favor from the One who knows how badly we need it. God can see all that junk and mess and dirt and all the stuff we're trying to hide. And He loves us anyway.

Let's go to Jesus now. Let's not wait another minute. He's here, and He's brought everything we need for a clean life. A wonderful life—in Him!

I thank You, Jesus, for Your mercy and grace! Amen. —A.H.

The Father of Heavenly Lights!

Every good and perfect gift is from above,
coming down from the Father of the heavenly lights,
who does not change like shifting shadows.

JAMES 1:17

You just meant to go for a short, quiet stroll, but the forest was deeper than you imagined and time got away from you. The sun is going down, and through the leaves, leftover bits of light dapple the dusky trail. Shadows crisscross here and there, shifting constantly around you. In no time, the ever-darkening patches fill with gloom, uncertainty, and fear. The tiniest breeze can change the shadows once again, so that you're no longer sure what is real or where you should go. So easily you become shrouded in darkness and utterly lost.

God promises us in His Word that He is not like shifting shadows. He is instead the Father of heavenly lights. God's character never changes from being holy. We can trust the Lord on this earthly path of ours. We can trust Him to give us good gifts. We can trust Him with His promises and with our very lives.

I am basking in Your radiant light, Lord! May I always
follow Your light and not the shifting shadows
offered by the enemy. Amen. —A.H.

We're Moving On

*But our citizenship is in heaven. And we eagerly
await a Savior from there, the Lord Jesus Christ.*
PHILIPPIANS 3:20

We get wrapped up so tightly in this life, we sometimes act as if this is all there is. We pray, "I would like good health all the time, a big house, a stellar career. I need grandkids, and great-grandkids, and a very long life to enjoy them, of course. I would very much like for all my family and friends to have long, good lives too. I want. . ."

And on and on and on. The Lord does indeed want us to take our requests to Him, but our list of demands would never end. Because some part of us wants to make this earth into heaven right now. In essence, we're not acting as if the kingdom of heaven is waiting for us.

This fallen world isn't the last stop on our journey. So when trouble comes to us, we can embrace the promise in Philippians 3:20—that as Christians our citizenship isn't here. Christ said He was going to prepare a place for us, and we can trust that He meant it!

*Lord, I thank You that I am an eternal being, and that
because of Your saving grace, I can spend all my
forevers with You in heaven! Amen. —A.H.*

Leap of Faith

*I will say of the LORD, "He is my refuge and
my fortress, my God, in whom I trust."*
PSALM 91:2

Most children love to jump fearlessly into their parents' waiting arms. They leap with the confidence of Superman, never looking back, focusing only on that glorious and soaring and laughing moment— that leap of faith into arms of love.

But what if you reached out to your child, and she backed away and said, "No way. You might tear my new shirt. You might look the other way and drop me. I'm too scared." Those words would no doubt confuse and pain you. This fearful response takes some of the glory and joy out of that trusting relationship, doesn't it?

Oh, how God wants us to trust Him as His beloved children! The Word says, "There is no fear in love. But perfect love drives out fear" (1 John 4:18 NIV). Do we love God enough to take that daily running leap into His arms? Do we trust Him with our very lives? That is what He expects—just like we would with our own children.

Have you taken that leap of faith into the arms of love?

*Lord, Lover of my soul, help me to
fearlessly trust in You. Amen. —A.H.*

So Much More

*Jesus replied, "All who love me will do what I say.
My Father will love them, and we will come
and make our home with each of them."*

JOHN 14:23 NLT

People are sometimes like those little spring-operated toys. Once they're wound up tightly and set free, they make some pretty crazy moves—jolting forward and then backward, zooming in eye-blurring circles, and then suddenly scuttling down the sidewalk to be run over by a tricycle!

We the people of this earth obviously need specific guidelines on how to live this life so we don't make those crazy, dangerous moves. God gave us His Word to show us the way to go, however, the Bible is so much more than a list of dos and don'ts. It shows us the history of salvation through Christ, and it also speaks to us through the power of His Holy Spirit. God wants to commune with us, to be with us. John revealed the Lord's desire for this intimate connection when he reported that Jesus even said He wanted to come and make His home with us. With each one of us.

Aren't you glad God sent us way more than a book of rules?

*Jesus, I thank You that You choose to
love me and dwell with me. Amen. —A.H.*

Stockpiling Mania

Then the LORD said to Moses, "I will rain down bread from
heaven for you. The people are to go out each day and
gather enough for that day. In this way I will test them
and see whether they will follow my instructions."

EXODUS 16:4

We love to stockpile—for those rainy days. It's in our nature. Those two-for-one sales on lip gloss aren't to be missed! So we buy in bulk, pack the attics like stuffed olives, and let a sea of storage facilities catch the overflow.

But sometimes God tests us—like the Israelites in the wilderness. God clearly said to them not to collect any more manna than was needed for one day, with the exception of gathering more before the Sabbath. But the people ignored God's instructions.

It's easy to say we trust God when we've got our cupboards packed with provisions. But it's harder to trust God day by day—for everything we need, spiritually, emotionally, and physically.

When the Lord says to wait, we should. If the Lord says to double up because a famine is coming, we should. We simply need to listen and trust in all matters. Difficult? Yes. Essential? Absolutely.

Lord, may I always listen carefully to You and
follow through with Your divine will! Amen. —A.H.

A Tug-of-War

"In everything I did, I showed you that by this kind of hard work we must help the weak, remembering the words the Lord Jesus himself said: 'It is more blessed to give than to receive.'"

ACTS 20:35

There is that moment's hesitation—a tug-of-war of sorts—either in our fingers or in our hearts, when we are not sure if we should offer that homeless man our money. After all, that money was hard-earned. And this homeless man is wearing some pretty nice sneakers. Is he just scamming people? Is he on drugs? Is he too lazy to work?

And yet, maybe this poor man has just fallen on hard times and needs someone to give him a helping hand. Maybe that someone is supposed to be you or me. So you let go of that money. The man's face lights up.

As you look in each other's eyes, you feel good, knowing that as you released your hold on that money, you released a little of God's generous love. And you know something else—if you found yourself out on the street and in need, you would hope some kind soul might remember Jesus' words and lose that tug-of-war.

Lord, as people cross my path, show me who
You would like me to bless. Amen. —A.H.

Who Is Worthy of Our Praise?

They traded the truth about God for a lie. So they worshiped and served the things God created instead of the Creator himself, who is worthy of eternal praise! Amen.
ROMANS 1:25 NLT

Why do we say God doesn't exist when our spirits cry out to Him? Perhaps this verse in Romans rings truer with every generation—that we have traded the truth about God for a lie.

The enemy of our souls—Satan—would like us to worship anything and everything besides the one true God. We might choose to worship science. Or perhaps some of the elements of creation, such as the moon and stars. Or we might even be tempted to think of ourselves as gods. Really? Us? Worthy of eternal praise? Or people might choose the religion of no religion at all. But do remember, everything we choose to believe in requires an element of faith!

Who do you choose to trust? Why not put your faith in the one true God, the lover of your soul? The One who sent His Son to live among us and die for us. Put your trust in Him and discover just how faithful He really is!

Lord God Almighty, I do believe in You. Help me to grow in my faith every day! In Jesus' name I pray. Amen. —A.H.

The Distant Journey

Your word is a lamp for my feet,
a light on my path.
PSALM 119:105

Every kind of newfangled flashlight imaginable has now flooded the marketplace. Like the itty-bitty ones that dangle off your keychain. Or the handy headlamp for spelunking under your kitchen sink. And there are the whopper ones, with enough light power to land a jet in your backyard!

We love illumination, don't we? Especially when it comes to the future.

We're resourceful at cooking up lots of questions too: Will I find a good husband? Will I be able to have kids? Will I ever move on from this going-nowhere job to a real career? Will I be stuck in this financial situation all my life? Will I age gracefully? Or not? These are valid questions, but God doesn't always give us the answers to all our life queries. He tends to offer us a lamp for the footpath in front of us—not necessarily a floodlight that shines well into the distant journey.

The Lord's way requires faith.

But just because God doesn't illuminate all of your journey right now doesn't mean He isn't attentive to all of your future.

Lord, help me to trust You for today's guidance
instead of demanding answers for the future.
In Jesus' name I pray. Amen. —A.H.

Better Than a Fairy Tale

By his divine power, God has given us everything we need for living a godly life. We have received all of this by coming to know him, the one who called us to himself by means of his marvelous glory and excellence. And because of his glory and excellence, he has given us great and precious promises. These are the promises that enable you to share his divine nature and escape the world's corruption caused by human desires.

2 PETER 1:3–4 NLT

From the moment we hear a fairy tale, we fall in love. These stories are full of princesses—who get to wear delectable gowns—and princes, castles, dastardly dragons, and noble deeds. They also give us some fantastical events and enchanting delights. But above all, when everything seems to be truly lost, in rides the white horse of happily-ever-afters. And isn't that what we long for most of all in our stories and in our lives?

In 2 Peter, the Lord offers us something far more wonderful than a storybook tale.

As we get to know Jesus, He gives us all we need to live a good and godly life. With His power, He will enable us to share in His divine nature. Imagine such precious pledges from our Lord!

Yes, fairy tales are fun, but God's promises are real and His happily-ever-afters are forever!

Thank You, Lord, for all my happily-ever-afters with You! Amen. —A.H.

The Puzzle

And we know that in all things God works for the good of those who love him, who have been called according to his purpose.
ROMANS 8:28

The jigsaw puzzle on the dining room table was beginning to come together. The lower corner was indeed looking more like the rounded shell of a turtle rather than your uncle Clyde's bald head. Then out of the blue, your new puppy scattered all the puzzle pieces like confetti on a windy day. Oy!

Does life ever feel that way? You were just beginning to see things coming together and then you're blindsided by some big event? Grief, illness, failure, adultery, depression, or a sudden lay-off. It becomes one of those moments when life seems confusing, random, and scary. It may even feel as though nothing good will ever happen to you again.

But God does promise to stay by our sides and work all things for good on our behalf. We may not get to see the puzzle in its final state on this side of eternity, but He will take that fearsome mess and transform it into something miraculous. Something beautiful.

We have His Word on it.

Lord, I don't understand what is happening to me right now, but I'm going to trust You in all things! Amen. —A.H.

When Your Heart Is Lonesome

Though my father and mother forsake me,
the LORD will receive me.

PSALM 27:10

Have you experienced the pain of abandonment or rejection in some form? Perhaps it came from a parent, a friend, a spouse, or another significant person in your life. The pain can leave you feeling lost, confused, depressed, and even frightened. It makes your heart lonesome when you realize that all you thought was secure and faithful wasn't as it seemed. You were instead subjected to the caprice of human nature. Unfortunately, it's the problem of living in a fallen world.

But your soul is calmed when you know that the Lord does not abandon His children. When people reject us, He welcomes and gathers us to Him. His ways are not selfish, but generous—not only giving with the riches of His love, but with the gift of His very life!

Yes, when your heart is lonesome, the Lord's arms are open. His love is real. His promises are forever. Take heart in the peace of God's faithfulness and prepare yourself to be loved!

Lord Jesus, I thank You that even when the whole world
seems to have abandoned me, You are there with
open arms. I am grateful that You will never leave
me or forsake me. I love You, Lord! Amen. —A.H.

Your Finest Friend

*There is no greater love than to lay
down one's life for one's friends.*
JOHN 15:13 NLT

Do you have a best friend? Someone you can talk to any time of the day or night? That 2 a.m. kind of friend who would do anything for you—and you'd do anything for her. You talk openly, lovingly, and frequently. You know her so well; you know what she'll say before she says it! You love each other better than life, you're closer than sisters, and you both trust each other no matter what. Now, that's a friendship worth far more than earthly treasures!

Isn't that just a little bit like the way we should feel about our relationship with God? But amazingly the Lord loves you even more than your best friend in her finest, most sacrificial hour. In fact, Christ loved you so much, He gave up His very life for you. Yes, that is a love and a friendship worth far more than earthly treasures! It's a friendship for all time.

*Thank You, Lord, for loving me so deeply. May I always
love You as dearly as You have loved me. Thank You for
friendship and fellowship. You have changed my life, both
for now and for all time! In Jesus' name I pray. Amen. —A.H.*

Walking on Water

"Come," he said. Then Peter got down out of the boat, walked on the water and came toward Jesus. But when he saw the wind, he was afraid and, beginning to sink, cried out, "Lord, save me!"
MATTHEW 14:29–30

We've all had those days when we started out on top of the stormy seas—walking with faith—but then at some point we succumbed to fears and doubts. Jesus summarizes the problem perfectly by saying, "The spirit is willing, but the flesh is weak" (Matthew 26:41).

Like Peter, you want to please the Lord, so you climb out of the boat—even in the midst of the whipping winds and the undulating waves that threaten to swallow you whole—and you start to walk on the water toward Him. It's a beautiful faith-filled moment! But maybe you experience a setback or some devastating news. Maybe you hear whispers from the enemy, of fearsome possibilities, and those doubts take hold of you. That's when you sink as Peter did.

The good news is that even if you've failed in faith, He is still there. If you cry out to Him, He will reach out His hand to you, rescue you, and restore you to Him!

Lord, when I sink, thank You for loving me still. In the future may my flesh be as willing as my spirit! Amen. —A.H.

His Simple Offering

"Here is a boy with five small barley loaves and two small fish, but how far will they go among so many?" Jesus said, "Have the people sit down." There was plenty of grass in that place, and they sat down (about five thousand men were there).
JOHN 6:9–10

The boy's face and hands may have been dusty. His offering was certainly small, but the mystery of faith had nudged at his heart, and he knew he must bring what he had to give. He pushed through the crowd toward the rabbi named Yeshua. The boy lifted up his basket of five small barley loaves and two fish to Yeshua, and this holy man of God smiled down at him. From that meager offering, that moment of simple faith, a crowd of thousands witnessed a miracle, as every belly was filled.

The whole world declares that bigger is better, more is magnificent. But God smiles at what we pass over as insignificant. The boy's offering wasn't about "how much," it was about his genuine desire to give.

How is our faith? Do we think our offering of money or talent or time is too meager? Try God. Give what you have and marvel at what a great God can do!

Lord, please take my daily offerings and use them to Your glory. Amen. —A.H.

Such Good and Lovely Things

Finally, brothers and sisters, whatever is true,
whatever is noble, whatever is right, whatever is pure,
whatever is lovely, whatever is admirable—if anything
is excellent or praiseworthy—think about such things.

Philippians 4:8

What are your favorite things? Miniature horses? Big chunks of cold, juicy watermelon on a hot day? Falling snowflakes and unfolding rosebuds? Harvest time and pumpkins rolling down the hill? Cooling breezes and laughter in the rain? Hummingbirds and nursing fawns? Delicate ferns on the forest floor? Silvery waterfalls cascading off the mountains?

God loves all these things too. In fact, He made them for your pleasure! What are some other things the Lord loves? Mercy and compassion, redemption and fellowship. Prodigals coming home. Hugs to welcome. Courage when facing fear. A life lived well with faith in Him. Justice won. Grace embraced. Songs of joy. A grateful heart, shouts of praise, offerings with a smile, encouraging words, and sharing the good news of Christ!

These are good and lovely and excellent things—not only as things to think about, but as a noble way to live one's life. A life of purpose and beauty and joy.

Lord, I thank You and praise You for all things
good and all things lovely! Amen. —A.H.

Miracles

*"I am the Lord, the God of all humankind.
Is anything too hard for me?"*
JEREMIAH 32:27

Even when the surface of life appears as still as a glassy sea, it is ever moving, ever changing, like a mighty undercurrent. And so it goes with the stirring hand of Providence.

People may not be able to see any divine intervention in the moment, but Christ-followers who love Him can be assured that God is always working things for good on their behalf. Some miracles are readily seen, some are not. Perhaps they will be made known years from now, or perhaps you will never know all the wonders that God has performed on this side of eternity.

Maybe you should keep a little book of miracles for each year so when you begin to feel nothing is changing, you can be reminded of all that God has done in your life. All the answered prayers you have forgotten. This will encourage your walk, your faith, your joy in Him.

Remember, the Lord is the God of all humankind. Nothing is too hard for Him.

*Thank You, Lord, for all You do in my life,
for miracles seen and unseen! Amen. —A.H.*

A Song from My Heart

GOD, brilliant Lord, your name echoes around the world.
PSALM 8:9 MSG

Who can stay unmoved in Your presence, Lord? Who can be silent seeing Your glory, which surrounds us all? You are majestic beyond anything we could have imagined! You have created such fathomless and breathtaking wonders!

How beautiful is Your name in all the earth! Indeed Your name echoes around the world. You are brilliant in all Your endeavors. Such marvels to behold, from the deepest oceans to the highest mountain summits, from the firmament's vast glory to the tiniest molecule under a microscope, we stand in awe of You and all the work of Your hands. All Your creation sings Your praises. We magnify Your name. We love You, and we worship You. We shout and sing for joy. We dance before You as Your servant David did. Praise and honor be Yours!

Lord, my God, may we always pleasure in and care for the beauty of Your elegantly made world. You alone are worthy of our sincerest love, our deepest devotion, and our enduring faith!

I love all that You've created, Lord. May it bring delight and joy to all who see it! And may it inspire humankind to seek the Giver of all these bountiful gifts. In Jesus' holy name I pray. Amen. —A.H.

Two Men, One Choice

One of the criminals who hung there hurled insults at him:
"Aren't you the Messiah? Save yourself and us!" But the other
criminal rebuked him. "Don't you fear God," he said, "since
you are under the same sentence? We are punished justly,
for we are getting what our deeds deserve. But this man has
done nothing wrong." Then he said, "Jesus, remember me
when you come into your kingdom." Jesus answered him,
"Truly I tell you, today you will be with me in paradise."
Luke 23:39–43

Life is full of daily choices. What to eat—broccoli or blueberry pie. What to wear—a sundress or a suit. What to do and say. "Will you marry me?"

But no choice will ever be as significant or as eternally important as deciding who Jesus Christ is to you and what you're going to do about it.

The two thieves on the cross with Jesus were faced with that same choice. One mocked Christ and the other repented. And at that moment, Jesus made a promise to the repentant man to take him to paradise. It doesn't get any clearer than that.

Two men on a cross, but one life-giving choice. Who do you trust with your life, your eternity?

Lord Jesus, forgive me for my sins. Thank You for Your sacrifice on
the cross. Please be my Lord and Savior. I'm looking forward to
someday living with You for all time! Amen. —A.H.

Leaky Faucet!

Knowledge flows like spring water from the wise;
fools are leaky faucets, dripping nonsense.
PROVERBS 15:2 MSG

Have you ever been with someone who is a living example of Proverbs 15:2? It may seem she has more words gushing out of her mouth than her tongue can safely handle. So much nonsensical gobbledygook, in fact, that your brain goes fuzzy, your eyes twitch, and all you can think about is how to turn off that rattling spigot! Was it a friend or coworker or family member or even a spouse? No? Surely the person wasn't you!

It's hard to get people to take us seriously when we spew folly all day. How will people trust us or respect us? How will they come to faith in Christ when we witness to them? Good questions, with only one answer. Pray that God will give us a new way of speaking. Proverbs also says, "They make a lot of sense, these wise folks; whenever they speak, their reputation increases" (16:23 MSG). Now, that sounds more like a Christian character we can welcome, befriend, respect, and trust. O Lord, please let it be so with us!

Lord, please control my tongue. Give me wisdom in all
areas of my life, including the words that flow out of
my mouth! In Jesus' name I pray. Amen. —A.H.

Sand and Stars

I will surely bless you and make your descendants as numerous as the stars in the sky and as the sand on the seashore.
GENESIS 22:17

He sat on top of a desert hill, looking up at the wide-open night sky. The moon shone bright, but dotted across the dark-blue blanket were millions of tiny white specks—a field seeded by tiny points of light. He lifted up his hand and let the fine grains of sand escape through his fingers. "As many as this?" Abraham's mind must have been spinning, thinking of all the children and children's children and generation after generation that would spread around the earth, pitching tents, constructing cities, exploring and filling the land.

His eyes wandered up to the high places on top of the mountain— the same mountain he had just climbed with his young son. Then his gaze settled on his son's peaceful face, as the boy rested. "Through you will the earth be blessed, my son," Abraham said to himself. "Never stop trusting that our Father God will provide everything we need—even when you don't know what might be waiting for you at the top of the mountain."

Father, help me to give everything to You, even when I don't want to let go, and when I can't understand. Amen. —M.L.

Laughter

Now the LORD was gracious to Sarah as he had said,
and the LORD did for Sarah what he had promised.
GENESIS 21:1

We tend to think of Sarah as this jovial old woman, lifting her newborn son into the air as she giggles in amazement at God's miraculous way of fulfilling all His promises. But Sarah had been through a lot of life by the time she had that beautiful baby boy.

How many times had the answers to her prayers not come—or at least, not in the way she thought that they might? How many times had she wondered what God was planning? How many times had she been disappointed or confused?

Is it really any wonder that she laughed at the idea of bearing a son in her old age? Wouldn't we scoff at the thought ourselves? Perhaps even laugh with a hint of bitterness?

But Sarah found out that truly, nothing is too hard for the Lord. And He always keeps His promises.

Abraham aptly named his son—for the first sound to fill those tiny, perfectly formed ears was the sound of laughter. It was the sound of the pure joy that comes from being reminded of the powerful love of God.

Dear Father of us all, I want to rejoice every day in the wonders
You have created for me. Help me to see them. Amen. —M.L.

Unless

*I tell you the truth, unless a kernel of wheat is planted in
the soil and dies, it remains alone. But its death will produce
many new kernels—a plentiful harvest of new lives.*

JOHN 12:24 NLT

The seeds sit in their dusty packets, waiting on the shelf for the
cold nights to be replaced by warm, spring breezes. Which ones
will get planted this year? Too bad their gardener is rather fickle
and forgetful—she may not even remember to plant any of them
until it is too late!

Each seed is like a little parcel of hope. It holds within it all the
information needed to create the plant that it is to become. All it
needs is a little water, a little warmth and light, some nutrients, and
then the instructions will unfurl. The cells will build and multiply
and stack themselves, one on top of another, until the stalk pokes
through the darkness and out into the sunlight.

And left behind in the wet earth, the precious case for this
cargo dies. Its job is done. Its work will produce a plant that will
grow and stretch and someday create seeds of its own.

Jesus served us all by dying for us—and through His death, all
of us may grow and step into the light, and tell others about the
hope to come.

*Thank You, Jesus, for dying so
that we may live! Amen.* —M.L.

Looking in the Wrong Place

"Don't dabble in the occult or traffic with mediums;
you'll pollute your souls. I am GOD, your God."
LEVITICUS 19:31 MSG

One leader surrounds himself with important people—people who have lots of money and power. But these people also have reputations, and they're not good ones. They are people who are cruel to those under them, who abuse their privileges, who take advantage of those who come to them for help.

Another leader can often be found in the company of scholars, creative thinkers, and service providers. She gathers information and inspiration from these people, who are known for their understanding, brilliance, and compassion.

We are often judged by who we go to for answers and guidance. It's easy to get caught up in a mystical experience that seems to promise much—psychics are practiced in the art of persuasion. But if we spend time with those who think they can find the answers on their own—by talking to the dead—our faith and our reputation will be polluted. If we focus instead on the Giver of all life and all knowledge, our faith and our witness to others will live on in His power.

God, help me remember that I don't need to go anywhere
else for answers—You are all I need. Amen. —M.L.

Building

*Now devote your heart and soul
to seeking the LORD your God.*
1 CHRONICLES 22:19

It was going to be a truly awesome work. The people were about to start preparations for creating the Temple of God—the place that would stand for more than four hundred years and be known as the dwelling place of the Almighty. The place where all who followed God would seek to come and give Him honor.

But before a hammer was lifted or a stitch sewn or a flake of gold melted, David challenged all the leaders of Israel who were going to help his son Solomon to focus—to commit, to promise, to give everything they had to seeking God's will.

Perhaps you are about to embark on a huge project. Perhaps you are at the start of a career, or a new fitness program, or an amazing ministry opportunity. Before you make a move, seek God's heart. Pray. Study His Word. Read the stories of His servants. Follow Jesus' steps. Ask for godly counsel. Give every part of your heart and mind over to understanding and loving Him.

Then you can begin your work—you can start your building. And you'll have the most solid foundation.

*God, thank You for being a rock-solid
place for me to stand on. Amen. —M.L.*

In Need of Rescue

He reached down from on high and took hold of me;
he drew me out of deep waters. He rescued me from my
powerful enemy, from my foes, who were too strong for me.
2 SAMUEL 22:17–18

Have you ever been in trouble in deep water? Something happens suddenly—a cramp, an accident, a moment of panic. And then you are stuck. And the more you flail and splash and reach for help, the more your body tires and your efforts seem only to feed your panic. You begin to go under. And each time you go under, it's just a little bit harder to get up again.

It seems impossible to make your limbs move in any helpful way. In most cases, the only way you are going to get out of this troubling, life-endangering situation, is to be in someone else's hands—literally.

Someone is going to have to pull you out.

We get stuck in life at times. It doesn't matter what the situation is—it may be a financial crisis, or a broken relationship, or a pit of sin that we can't crawl out of—but at some point we have to acknowledge that there is no way we are going to get ourselves out. We need help. Who do you call on for help?

Lord, thank You for rescuing me. Amen. —M.L.

Into His Hands

Into your hands I commit my spirit;
deliver me, LORD, my faithful God.
PSALM 31:5

When you hear the words of Psalm 31, what do you think of? Many people who are followers of Jesus would say that they think of Jesus on the cross. These words were the ones Jesus cried out just before He "breathed his last" (Luke 23:46).

In the verse just before this one, verse 4, the psalmist asks the Lord to "keep me free from the trap that is set for me, for you are my refuge." One wonders what the trap might have been for this writer. He later speaks of an "affliction" that makes him "an object of dread," even to the people who love him the most.

Maybe you are in an equally dire situation. Maybe you feel trapped. Or maybe you have even been confronted with the thought that you will have to face death soon. But you don't have to be facing death, and you don't have to be an object of dread before you commit your spirit to God's hands.

Whatever stage of life you are in and wherever you are in your journey of faith, you can say these words: "I commit my spirit to You, Lord." God is faithful. If you give your life to Him, He will save you.

Dear Lord, I commit my spirit to You now. Amen. —M.L.

The Faith of the Centurion

"But just say the word, and my servant will be healed."
MATTHEW 8:8

The centurion we meet in Matthew's account is a fascinating man. He was a professional officer of the Roman army, and he would have had at least a hundred men under his charge, although in practice a "century" of soldiers might contain two hundred to one thousand men.

Historical records tell us that centurions did not order their men into battle from some safe vantage point. They were right beside their men, fighting with them—sometimes even going first. They led by example, and generally showed great skill and great courage.

So when this man came to Jesus, all eyes would have been on him. *He's an important man*, people might have thought, *Why is he talking to this teacher from Nazareth?*

True to military form, the centurion gets straight to the point: he tells Jesus about his servant, who is "suffering terribly" (v. 6). Then Jesus offers to come to his house. But the centurion—this leader of men and elite warrior—says no. "Just give me the orders," he seems to say instead. "Just say the word." And so Jesus does. And the servant is healed.

Amazing things happen when we truly believe in the power of Jesus. Not everyone will be healed in the moment, but everyone will become better.

Lord, just say the word. I'm listening. Amen. —M.L.

As Surely

"As surely as the sun rises, he will appear; he will come to us like the winter rains, like the spring rains that water the earth."

HOSEA 6:3

When it's a cloudy day, or when the fog rolls in, everything seems to be touched by a shade of gray. Houses are a little grayer. Flowers are a little droopier.

And when the weather forecast is not so sunny and bright, we can feel a little gray too. But the good thing is we can always depend on the weather to change.

However, one thing is for certain. When the sun is blocked by clouds, or by an eclipse, or indeed, when it runs away each night to a different side of the world, we don't suddenly believe the sun is never returning. We don't lament its absence. We don't give up hope.

Why? Because we know that the next day, and the next, and the next, the sun is going to be there. It will rise once again in the east, and set again in the west. It's a sure thing.

And so is God. He will come to us, over and over again. So when it seems like He is not there, or when our days are looking a little dark, have faith. Don't despair. As surely as there is sunshine and rain, God will be with us.

Thank You for being even more sure than the sun. Amen. —M.L.

A Worthy Partner

Barak said to her, "If you go with me, I will go;
but if you don't go with me, I won't go."
JUDGES 4:8

Do you ever wonder what Deborah was like? She must have been a pretty amazing woman—the kind who could be just as happy wearing heels or combat boots. The kind of woman that people like to lean on in times of trouble.

After all, Deborah was a leader of Israel. She held court under the Palm of Deborah (she even had a tree named for her!) and when any of the Israelites were fighting, they would go to her to have their disputes resolved. Oh, to have been a fly on the trunk of that palm! The stories Deborah must have heard could have made for some excellent TV, for sure.

But not only was she wise and decisive, she was mighty. Barak is meant to be the leader of ten thousand men. Ten thousand! Deborah doesn't just send this commander on his way—she tells him that she herself is going to lead the enemy army into Barak's hands.

And Barak agrees to the plan, because Deborah is going to be his partner. When you are faithful to God, God is faithful to you. And everyone is drawn to that kind of power.

Lord, help me to be as wise and
strong as Deborah. Amen. —M.L.

Deceitful Hearts

The heart is hopelessly dark and deceitful, a puzzle that no one can figure out. But I, God, search the heart and examine the mind. I get to the heart of the human. I get to the root of things.
JEREMIAH 17:9–10 MSG

This passage might readily come to mind right after a person has been dumped. And certainly, it might be used as a description of the one who did the dumping. "What a jerk! His heart is hopelessly dark and deceitful—how in the world was I supposed to know what he was feeling?"

Our hearts do puzzle us. Feelings fool us. One day we have a deep longing to follow after God—and on another day we have a deep longing for goat cheese and artichoke pizza. Who can figure us out?

At first glance, this verse sounds hopelessly dark itself. But the hope comes, as it often does, with the *but*. "But I, God." Now there is certainly something scary about the idea of God searching our hearts and examining our thoughts. But there's something comforting in it too. Because if we let God do this, if we allow Him to root out our deceptions and bring our true selves to the light, well, there's nowhere to go but up, right?

Thank You, Lord, for searching my heart. Amen. —M.L.

Living through Him

This is how God showed his love among us: He sent his one and only Son into the world that we might live through him.

1 JOHN 4:9

Such a small verse—such a big message!

"That we might live through him"—those words should give us a thrill. What an amazing God we have that He was willing to offer His own Son's life as a sacrifice, just so we could live with Him.

This kind of "living through" is not some version of vicarious experience—like when we see our friend's Hawaii trip pictures online and pretend we are in each one. It is not that we can imagine living life as Jesus did in first-century Jerusalem. We live through Him because the only way that we can live forever, the only way we can escape the punishment of death for our sins, the only way we can really live at all, is by faith in Jesus.

Lord, thank You for Your great love. Thank You for the sacrifice of Your Son. I can't imagine loving anyone like that. But You, Lord, gave up everything for us. Help me to understand that more. Amen. —M.L.

The Ticket

If you declare with your mouth, "Jesus is Lord," and believe in your heart that God raised him from the dead, you will be saved.

ROMANS 10:9

The doors closed just as her ticket was whooshed out of her sweaty fingers and down onto the concrete. Too late. Her ticket was gone.

As the ticket attendant made his way down the gently swaying aisle, she became nervous. What would he do? She didn't have any more money. Would he throw her out?

He approached her to stamp her ticket. She declared that she had bought her ticket and had it in her hand, but now it was gone. She looked up at him with an honest face and promised that she had most definitely bought a ticket for that train.

Now, if the attendant had been like God, that's all that would have been required. But too bad, he wasn't much like God. He booted the girl off the train at the next stop. This man was a rule follower, not a grace giver, and he needed that ticket.

You've got a ticket in to heaven. All you have to do is match your words to what is in your heart, and proclaim that Jesus is Lord. Can you do that today?

Lord, I declare that You are Lord of my heart,
now and always. Amen. —M.L.

A Tower of a Woman

After this, Jesus traveled about from one town and village to another, proclaiming the good news of the kingdom of God. The Twelve were with him, and also some women who had been cured of evil spirits and diseases: Mary (called Magdalene) from whom seven demons had come out. . . . These women were helping to support them out of their own means.

LUKE 8:1–3

Jesus included women in His ministry in a way no man ever had then, and at first glance in these verses, you might just see a list of women. But look closer.

There was Mary (called Magdalene, whose name means "tower"), who had been healed from having seven demons. If you read very much in the Bible, you'll see that having even one demon was enough to cause an individual significant harm. The fact that Mary had seven demons in her and lived to tell about it shows both the power of Christ and the physical and mental strength of this woman. In other accounts about Mary, she is also referred to as a prostitute. In other words, her life had not been an easy one.

But here she is, following Jesus, supporting Jesus' work. Later, she would be one of the first voices to announce Jesus' resurrection. Only the power and grace of Jesus designs such stories.

*Lord, I want to be a strong witness for You.
Help me to speak about You wherever I go. Amen. —M.L.*

Not an Easy Job

*"You will be hated by everyone because of me,
but the one who stands firm to the end will be saved."*
MATTHEW 10:22

It's not exactly a job most people would run to sign up for, is it? Wanted: Men and women to follow a teacher at all costs. You will be subject to name-calling, rejection, hatred, and persecution of various kinds (possibly including bodily harm and loss of life). You will be paid no money, and your work will not be recognized by most people. But after you die, you will live forever in heaven.

That last line is the kicker. But how many people never get to that last line?

Jesus says that His followers will be hated by everyone. It seems He probably meant all kinds of people from various backgrounds will find reasons to hate what Christians do. We certainly see that happening today. In fact, churches and Christian organizations often do their best to try to hide their "Christian-ness" in the ways they promote events and programming—to get over that first hurdle of hate. In our society perhaps hatred has been replaced by annoyance or indifference. If we could just get past those barriers, we might have a chance at reaching people. But in any case, we who follow Jesus must keep standing firm. Only then will we get the real and best reward—eternity with Him.

*Lord God, I don't want people to hate me, but I
never want to leave You. Help me stay. Amen. —M.L.*

Guided into the Truth

*"When he, the Spirit of truth, comes,
he will guide you into all the truth."*
JOHN 16:13

Much about walking in the footsteps of Jesus can be confusing. Sometimes it is just difficult, in the chorus of voices that we hear every day, to understand who is speaking the truth and who isn't.

It is comforting to know that, as we walk this path of faith, we don't go it alone. We have others here on earth who can guide us through their wisdom and experience. But we also have an even greater guide—Jesus says we have the Spirit of truth.

You may have felt the Spirit's guidance in all kinds of situations. The Spirit might raise in you an awareness of injustice. Or maybe the Spirit leads you to a good source for understanding certain scriptures. Or perhaps the Spirit has convicted you about a lack of truth in your life.

The Spirit speaks in many ways. The only trick is that we do have to listen.

*Lord Jesus, help me to look for and listen to and
celebrate the Spirit of truth in my life. Amen. —M.L.*

Little Imitators

*Therefore be imitators of God, as beloved children,
and live in love, as Christ loved us and gave himself
up for us, a fragrant offering and sacrifice to God.*
EPHESIANS 5:1–2 NRSV

The little boy followed along after his big brother, matching step for step. When his brother jumped, the little legs jumped. When his brother zigged, so did his shadow. And when his naughty brother jumped in the mud puddle—well, you can just guess what happened next. Mom had some laundry to do, that's for sure.

Children love to imitate the special big people in their lives. It's an important part of their development—a vital path of learning. They learn to speak by listening to our voices and watching our mouths. They learn to eat by watching us eat—usually like a hawk! They learn to obey (or not) by observing us too.

Besides these key components of early learning, children also pick up on things like kindness, generosity, compassion, sorrow, forgiveness, worry, anger, and love. If you are a parent, this list may well strike fear in your heart. *My kid is going to learn all that from me?* The good thing is, Jesus gave us someone to imitate as well—Him! And since He's the perfect example, if we follow Him, we can't go wrong.

*Thank You for providing the perfect
example of how to live. Amen. —M.L.*

She's Not Heavy

*Bear one another's burdens, and in
this way you will fulfill the law of Christ.*
GALATIANS 6:2 NRSV

The elderly woman stooped over her pull-cart of packages, arranging things one last time before she tried to tackle the escalator. Anyone watching the scene probably could have anticipated the accident that was about to happen. The lady with the packages wrestled with the cart to get it on the edge of the first escalator step, but before she could find her footing, the steps sped away from her. The cart fell forward, and she fell backward—right onto the unsuspecting shopper behind her. The shopper did the only thing she could do. She stood as firm and strong as a pillar, supporting the woman's weight. Later the shopper told a friend that for such a tiny, frail-looking thing, that old woman must have been built like a brick!

Perhaps the shopper might have wanted to change the words of the classic song to "She *is* heavy, and she *ain't* my sister! Someone get her off me!"

We are to bear one another's burdens, whether they are heavy and many or few and light. None of us is exempt from this duty. So be prepared! You never know when someone's burdens, or someone, might land right in your lap.

God, make me strong so I can hold others up. Amen. —M.L.

Overlooking

*A person's wisdom yields patience;
it is to one's glory to overlook an offense.*
PROVERBS 19:11

Proverbs is a book filled with wisdom for our faith journeys. Every Christian should read the wise words held in those pages from time to time and memorize key passages. This verse in Proverbs 19 is definitely a key scripture for those who are trying to walk out their faith.

Do you want to know what causes most of the problems in today's churches? The answer is right here in Proverbs 19:11. People just can't seem to let things go. They run out of patience quickly with one another, and then—*wham!* Someone says something snarky, another person answers back in defense, and before you know it, lines are drawn and sides are picked and divisions are born.

But here we see the truth of how we are to live. The real result that could come from right behavior and patient reflection. "It is to one's glory to overlook an offense."

Do you really want to win some points in the eyes of God? Don't worry about being on the "right" side. Be on the side of glory.

Lord, we do so many things wrong in our churches today. We hurt and insult and offend one another. And in doing so, we present a picture of strife and discord to those on the outside looking in. Help us to be patient, Lord. Forgive us. Amen. —M.L.

In Him All Things

He is before all things, and in him all things hold together.
COLOSSIANS 1:17

Sometimes people get confused between what God *does* and who God *is*. For example, God makes things. He has made our universe and the planet on which we are now sitting. He's made the flowers and trees, and the monkeys that swing from the branches and the monkeys that wrestle on our playroom floors. He's made everything we see, and a great many things that are invisible to our eyes. And He's made you and me.

But God is God. God is not the universe. God is not this planet. God is not the flowers and trees, or the monkeys and bees. God is not you, and God is certainly not me.

He cannot both be created and Creator—He was before all this ever came to be. Yet it is only through Him and in His power that this delicate balance we call life is held together.

Do you sometimes feel closer to God when you focus on a forget-me-not or stare up into the branches of a mighty oak? Of course!—God's hands have been in all of it, and He has uniquely reconciled all things to Him, making peace with every part of His creation through the blood of His Son.

Lord, thank You for holding us all together
in this beautiful jumble of life. Amen. —M.L.

Martha's Complaint

"Lord," Martha said to Jesus, "if you had
been here, my brother would not have died."
JOHN 11:21

How many times do you think Martha's words will be echoed in hospital hallways this week? "God, where were You?" "Lord, I prayed. Why didn't You come? Why didn't You heal him?" "Jesus, I need You here—now. If You could just be here, I know everything would be okay. I know You could fix everything."

"God, why?"

When something hard happens, and especially when we lose someone we love, the pain and grief is often so strong that it's very difficult for us to see anything else. We don't see the quiet support of those who pray for us. We don't feel the hands of those who are holding us up. We can't imagine the plans that have been put into place so we don't fall apart.

But rest assured, Jesus knows your sorrow. And He gives us this hope, "The one who believes in me will live, even though they die; and whoever lives by believing in me will never die" (vv. 25–26).

Do you believe that?

Lord, help me to rest in the confidence that You are with me and
that You have my loved ones in Your safe hands. Amen. —M.L.

No Captives

See to it that no one takes you captive through hollow and deceptive philosophy, which depends on human tradition and the elemental spiritual forces of this world rather than on Christ.
Colossians 2:8

If you can think of it, there's probably an "ism" for it. John Dewey, a philosopher and education reformer once said, "Any movement that thinks and acts in terms of an 'ism becomes so involved in reaction against other 'isms that it is unwittingly controlled by them."

We let this happen to the church too often. It can happen quite slowly over time. Writers write books, and people buy them and recommend them and share them. And before you know it, the church gets further and further away from the Bible, and more and more confused as to what God actually said, and more worried about how a handful of authors have interpreted His words.

Certainly, we should read books. And we should promote good authors. But we also regularly need to immerse ourselves in the language and thoughts of the Word of God. We need to be more concerned with taking captive our thoughts, than with the captivating voices of popular movements.

Lord, fill our minds with solid and truthful reasoning from Your Word. Amen. —M.L.

The Trouble with Anger

My dear brothers and sisters, take note of this:
Everyone should be quick to listen, slow to speak
and slow to become angry, because human anger
does not produce the righteousness that God desires.
JAMES 1:19–20

For quite some time now, the idea has been tossed around that it's important for everyone to express themselves. It's important to let it all out. No one should repress their emotions or outbursts. We should not control our impulses, but instead release them in healthy ways.

But none of that is in God's Word. God acknowledges the full range of human emotions and expressions. But He tells us to have self-control. Why?

The simple answer is right here in the letter from James: "Human anger does not produce the righteousness that God desires." If we want to become more like God, if we want to become the flourishing human beings God created us to be, then we have to give up the idea that all expressions of emotion are good.

Anger hurts. Anger masks. Anger almost never lets you get to the real point of things. Anger keeps us from coming to resolutions and bringing peace into our lives. And isn't that what we want in the end?

Lord, thank You for reminding us of what is
true and important for us to grow. Amen. —M.L.

Inside and Out

God hasn't invited us into a disorderly,
unkempt life but into something holy and beautiful—
as beautiful on the inside as the outside.
1 THESSALONIANS 4:7 MSG

Have you ever had unexpected company? Perhaps you are one of those blessed souls who always manages to keep her home neat and tidy. But if you are not one of those abnormal—um, I mean unique—people, you might be scrambling to shove laundry in the oven and newspapers under the couch cushions while your guest is walking up the driveway.

This verse, of course, is not talking about an orderly house, but about an orderly soul. It's part of a passage that addresses the purity of the listeners—challenging the audience to keep their bodies pure and to avoid sexual immorality. Apparently this is a subject that Paul has had to address with the Thessalonians on other occasions (see v. 6). But is that surprising? One wonders how many letters on sexual immorality Paul would have to write to our churches today if he were alive to do so. He'd probably need to write a daily blog about it.

Sexual immorality is more than just a sin involving your body. It affects your purity of mind and spirit as well. It can disorder your thoughts and mess up your goals. We should value our bodies, and our whole selves, more than that.

Dear Lord, please help me make my life
beautiful inside and out. Amen. —M.L.

What Is Good

He has shown you, O mortal, what is good. And what does the LORD require of you? To act justly and to love mercy and to walk humbly with your God.

MICAH 6:8

The clarity of the prophets' words can be so encouraging at times. Here Micah shows us exactly what we need to do to be good. He tells us clearly what God requires.

To act justly. We are to treat people as we would want to be treated. We are to take care of those who can't take care of themselves, and to make sure that those in power are making decisions that consider the weakest members of our society.

To love mercy. We are to forgive before being asked. We are to be generous with what we have, and show even our enemies a love they can't fathom. We are to seek out ways to extend God's mercy and grace to everyone we know.

To walk humbly with God. We must never boast about the good that we do, but instead, we should always be aware that we can do nothing, be nothing, serve no one, except that God has allowed us to do so. We must become less, and He must become greater.

Lord, I understand what You want me to do.
Help me to do it. Amen. —M.L.

The Power of Love

"Where you go I will go, and where you stay I will stay.
Your people will be my people and your God my God."
RUTH 1:16

Perhaps Naomi was blinded by grief. Or maybe she was just too wrapped up in her own bitterness and disappointment to see. But she almost missed out on the best in-law relationship ever.

When her sons and her husband had succumbed to illness and died, Naomi just wanted to go home, to her own country. She urged her sons' widows to go back to their families. But Ruth wouldn't go. Perhaps she didn't have anything to go back to. But Ruth pledged herself to her mother-in-law and begged Naomi to let her stay with her.

Naomi relented, and through the relationship established via Naomi's family and by Ruth's good character, Ruth wed Boaz and then gave birth to Obed. And from the line of Obed eventually came David. And from the line of David, came Jesus Christ.

When someone shows their good character and asks to remain in relationship, give them a chance. You may just be living out a very special part of God's perfect plan.

Lord, help me not to be blind to holy relationships that You are placing in front of me. Help me to extend grace whenever I can, and to offer friendship, even when I don't feel like it. Amen. —M.L.

Open Your Heart

The Lord opened her heart to respond to Paul's message.
ACTS 16:14

The Bible account tells us this about Lydia: "One of those listening was a woman from the city of Thyatira named Lydia, a dealer in purple cloth. She was a worshiper of God" (Acts 16:14).

Have you been going through the motions, attending church, singing songs, praying prayers, doing projects, but not really giving your life over to God? Open your heart.

Have you been opposed to taking that extra step to be baptized and commit yourself publicly to following the way of Jesus, and yet you can't really think of a good reason why? Open your heart.

Have you hung back while others stepped forward to ask for prayer, even though you have a burden weighing heavily on your soul? Open your heart.

Have you come up with a million excuses why you can't do service projects, while you know the only reason you really have is that you are just afraid to work with people who are so different from you? Open your heart.

The life of faith was never meant to be lived in fear. Take courage. Follow Lydia's example. Let God open your heart.

Lord, reveal to me the areas in my life where I've been holding back from being fully committed to You. Open my heart. Amen. —M.L.

Don't Judge?

"Do not judge, or you too will be judged. For in the same way you judge others, you will be judged, and with the measure you use, it will be measured to you."

MATTHEW 7:1–2

There's a lot of confusion in the church on this point, and it can cause breakdowns in communications between believers.

One definition of judging is the idea of forming a negative opinion about someone, without complete or reliable information. This is what people mean when they say something like, "I just ate my ninth donut today. Don't judge." They don't want you to form a negative opinion about them, as people, based on this one day of bad eating.

Fair enough (says the writer who just had whipped cream and sugar put in her coffee).

Another meaning for the verb *judge* is to form an opinion about something through careful deliberation—looking into the evidence and making a decision based on the best information available.

This is what someone means when they say, "You can read about the candidates and what they stand for here. Then judge which one will make the best representative." This is not about forming a negative opinion—this is making an informed decision.

We must make reasoned, informed decisions all the time. But we must keep our ill-informed, negative opinions to ourselves.

Lord, help us to judge fairly and with Your wisdom. Amen. —M.L.

Forgiven Much

*"Her many sins have been forgiven—as her great love
has shown. But whoever has been forgiven little loves little."*
LUKE 7:47

As we come together to worship our Lord and Savior, we must remember one important thing: we have been forgiven much.

Whenever we feel tempted to think of ourselves as better than someone else, we need to remember: we have been forgiven much.

When we don't feel like reading the Bible or praying or having self-control, we should remember: we have been forgiven much.

And because we have been forgiven much, now is the time to kneel at our Savior's feet, and kiss Him, and bless Him, and serve Him.

In this story in Luke 7, Simon, the Pharisee who was supplying the feast, was upset. This woman was a known sinner—why should she be given any attention?

But Jesus quickly put him in his place: "Do you see this woman? I came into your house. You did not give me any water for my feet, but she wet my feet with her tears and wiped them with her hair." Can you feel the amazing love this woman poured out on her Lord?

Can you see how much we owe Him? We have been forgiven much.

*Dear Lord and Savior Jesus Christ, help me remember
how much I have been forgiven. Amen. —M.L.*

More Religion

Religion that God our Father accepts as pure and faultless is this: to look after orphans and widows in their distress and to keep oneself from being polluted by the world.

JAMES 1:27

The word *religion* has become a negative word to many people. When they hear it, they think of divisions, wars, suffering, cruelty, inquisitions, restrictions, abuse, corruption, politics, and discrimination. The concept has certainly become polluted by its many connections to negative events and powerful institutions.

But Jesus still means love to almost everyone around the world.

Our challenge as faithful followers of our Lord is to be His hands and feet in the world today. And James has given us a concept of pure and faultless religion: taking care of those who have been left on their own in distress, through no fault of their own. The mission in such cases is clear—there's no misunderstanding. We are called to take care of those who have no power, no voice, no resources. We are called to provide and love, to be in effect the new family for those who have lost their spouses and parents and siblings and friends.

So, what do you say? Do you want more of that religion in your life?

Lord, help us, Your followers, to not be confused about what we are doing here. Help us to stay focused on the people who need Your love. Amen. —M.L.

Whom Will You Serve?

"Choose for yourselves this day whom you will serve, whether the gods your ancestors served beyond the Euphrates, or the gods of the Amorites, in whose land you are living. But as for me and my household, we will serve the LORD."
JOSHUA 24:15

It would seem that humans just keep coming up with new things to worship and idolize every day. Some people think it doesn't really matter what or who you worship, as long as you acknowledge a higher power. They reason that as long as you can focus on something outside yourself, you'll be a better person.

But only the one true God can lead us away from ourselves and to the truth. In all other religions, people eventually get caught up in worshipping themselves again, because there is no absolute, supreme authority that exists on its own in those systems, and no gods that have not in some way been created or shaped by human hands or human ideas.

The Lord our God is the King of kings and the Lord of lords. Yahweh is the Alpha and the Omega, the Beginning and the End. The Word. The Light. The Way. There is no one like our God.

So, choose for yourself. Whom will you serve?

Thank You, Lord, for who You are. Amen. —M.L.

Loneliness

Turn to me and be gracious to me,
for I am lonely and afflicted.
PSALM 25:16

Some people think that when they follow Jesus they will never feel lonely again. What a friend we have in Jesus—He's always there for us! And this is true. Jesus is always with us, and He is our friend in the sense that He supports us and loves us. But He's not going to hang out at the movies with us and eat popcorn. And sometimes He doesn't return our texts right away.

Face it, we are human beings with human bodies and human feelings. And until we have been changed into immortals, we are probably always going to feel the human need for companionship. And that's completely normal. It's even good. It's that desire to be with other humans that pushes us to reach out and talk to people. It leads us into new opportunities to show God's love.

But God understands loneliness. Consider Jesus in the garden at Gethsemane or God in the garden of Eden after the man and woman had to be put out.

And what's more, God understands our feelings because He is the one who created our feelings. He put these human hearts and minds in our human bodies. He knows what we need before we can even put words to it.

So if you are feeling lonely, go to God. Talk to Him. And then go out and find some other humans.

Dear Lord, thank You for understanding
us so completely. Amen. —M.L.

All Stumble

We all stumble in many ways.
JAMES 3:2

This particular verse should be required reading for every one of us who belongs to the Klutz Club. We know all about stumbling. And falling. And bruising.

But that's not the kind of stumbling James was talking about. In verse 1, James says, "Not many of you should become teachers, my fellow believers, because you know that we who teach will be judged more strictly." And then in verse 2, James points out that "anyone who is never at fault in what they say is perfect, able to keep their whole body in check."

We all mess up. But those of us who are in positions of leadership, especially those who have been called to teach young minds, must realize that we have more eyes on us than the rest of the crowd. Everyone should be held accountable, but teachers are not just leaders while they are in the classroom—their students watch how they live their lives.

So what can we do? How can we balance this knowledge that everyone makes mistakes, but some are held to a higher standard? We must approach our leaders and teachers with grace and love and encouragement. We should speak out when we see inappropriate behavior, but we should also offer forgiveness and grace.

In other words, we should treat them like Jesus would.

Lord, help me to support the teachers
and leaders in my area. Amen. —M.L.

Down

Why are you down in the dumps, dear soul? Why are you crying the blues? Fix my eyes on God—soon I'll be praising again.
PSALM 42:5 MSG

It could be for all the right reasons or no reason at all. It could be because of a loss, a disappointment, or a crushing defeat. It could attack because you just can't get your hair to behave, or it could visit you during a funeral, or even in the middle of a joyous concert crowd.

Depression can strike all kinds of people at different times in different ways.

True depression is a medical condition. It is a mental disorder. A dysfunction of the mind and body. It isn't just a passing feeling or "having a bad day."

And people with depression can't just get over it. Not without help and treatment.

God made us. He made us to be perfectly formed, but He understands that we are not perfect. He understands our sicknesses, our sufferings, our hurts, and our heartaches.

Will fixing our eyes on God cure depression? No, maybe not. But can focusing on someone who loves us so much He gave up everything so we can live with Him make a difference to the state of our souls? Yes, it sure can.

Please Lord, help me to fix my eyes on You. Amen. —M.L.

Known

In Joppa there was a disciple named Tabitha (in Greek her name is Dorcas); she was always doing good and helping the poor.
ACTS 9:36

She doesn't get many verses, certainly not a full chapter. But she is mentioned all the same. And in the few words that make up the story of this woman named Tabitha (or Dorcas), we find out some important things.

She was a disciple, a student of the teachings of Jesus Christ.

Tabitha had a good heart, and she put her good character into action. She lived what she was learning. She did what she could for those who were struggling around her.

Tabitha was loved. She was so loved, that when she became sick and then died, her body was carefully taken care of and placed in a special room, a room to show her significance. She was so loved, two men were sent to rush off and get the apostle Peter. "Please come at once!" (v. 38).

She was missed. In the short time she had been gone, a crowd had gathered. The widows cried—Tabitha had been their friend and supporter. Tabitha had encouraged them with her kind acts. Now she was gone, the simple clothes she had made were treated like treasures.

What will you be known for when you are gone? Whose lives are you touching today?

Dear Lord, help me to live a life of
love and generosity. Amen. —M.L.

Let It Go

"And when you stand praying, if you hold anything against anyone, forgive them, so that your Father in heaven may forgive you your sins."

MARK 11:25

You know what it's like. You're standing there in church. You've got your righteous outfit on. You've got your holiest heels. And you are loving the music this morning.

Then it comes time for prayer and you finally have a moment to think. You couldn't help but notice that the woman who cut you off on the road the other day is standing *right down there* at the end of your row.

The nerve. *Why is she even here?* you think. Clearly the woman isn't a Christian, right? I mean, she's certainly at the very least an awful driver.

Then you notice something else. She's pregnant. And alone. And she's quietly crying.

Wow, she must be struggling. I wonder if her husband just doesn't come? Or maybe she doesn't have a husband?

And suddenly you know what you're supposed to do. But it seems so weird. *Forgive her? Go to her? Is that really what You want from me, God?*

That's really what He wants. Forgive as He has forgiven you. Let go of the anger. Let go of the grudge. Let go of the justification. Let go of the self-interest. Let it all go. Just forgive.

Lord, show me who I need to forgive, and help me do it. Amen. —M.L.

Joy!

The LORD is my strength and my shield; my heart
trusts in him, and he helps me. My heart leaps
for joy, and with my song I praise him.
PSALM 28:7

The little girl dances to the music coming from the open shop door.
She twists and twirls, letting her wide skirt spin all around her. Her
curls bounce on her head as she hops and skips and leaps into the
air. This is a picture of pure joy!

Way too often, Christians are associated with somber faces and
serious hearts. The Bible tells us there is a time to laugh and a time
to dance too—so why so serious?

Maybe we fear judgment. Maybe we think if we aren't sober,
someone might think we are being too frivolous. Maybe we just
think too much.

It's time to show the world the joy of the Lord. What can you
do to show joy in your life today? Maybe you could throw a block
party or treat someone to the movies. Maybe take a bunch of kids
on a picnic or spontaneously break into song.

Whatever you do, have fun doing it!

God of my joy, help my life be a delight in Your eyes.
Help me not to take myself too seriously. Amen. —M.L.

It Only Takes a Spark

*Consider what a great forest
is set on fire by a small spark.*

JAMES 3:5

Sometimes our faith feels so fragile, doesn't it? The tiniest crack can cause our whole world to crumble. One little whispered secret, one little unkind word, one little white lie, one little bitter complaint, and suddenly the whole foundation of our little faith seems to be on shaky ground.

It doesn't take much to cause major destruction.

The tongue is a powerful tool. We can lift others up with it—showering people with praise and offering encouragement. But we can also tear people down—voicing negativity and complaints and criticisms. Or even worse. Sometimes just a few thoughtless words can bring a person's reputation under scrutiny, which then leads to job loss, financial ruin, and family stress and divorce. And it could all begin with just a few words.

James cautions us that "no human being can tame the tongue. It is a restless evil, full of deadly poison" (v. 8). Then what can we do? How can we fight to control the damage our tongues can inflict? The answer comes a bit later in this chapter—it comes through embracing peace-loving wisdom. We just have to keep working at it.

*Almighty Father, help me to control
my unruly tongue. Amen. —M.L.*

Entrusted

His master replied, "Well done, good and faithful servant!
You have been faithful with a few things; I will put you in charge
of many things. Come and share your master's happiness!"
MATTHEW 25:21

Jesus used stories called parables to teach many things about what the kingdom of God was like and what the world would be like at the end. He told the people stories about situations they could understand, probably in hopes that they would remember these stories better.

In Matthew 25, Jesus gives three images of what the relationship between God and His people will be like at the time of judgment. In one story, He offers up the idea of a man who went on a journey, leaving his wealth entrusted to three servants. Two of the servants doubled their master's wealth. When the master returned, he praised them for being "good and faithful." But one servant could only return what he had been given, because he had been too afraid to use his master's money. That servant was thrown out "into the darkness, where there will be weeping and gnashing of teeth" (v. 30).

God has entrusted us with His kingdom. He has entrusted us with one another. What will we have to show our Master when He returns? What are we doing today to expand our Master's kingdom?

Lord, I humbly offer my life to You. Help me
to expand Your kingdom. Amen. —M.L.

The Good Fight

*Fight the good fight for the true faith. Hold tightly to
the eternal life to which God has called you, which
you have declared so well before many witnesses.*
1 TIMOTHY 6:12 NLT

Have you ever heard people describe a boxing competition as
a "good fight"? Not much seems good about two guys beating
each other up so their faces are battered and bleeding. But when
the strength and skills of the sparring partners are well matched,
the competition is good in the sense that each lands some good
punches, the two learn from each other, and they are made better
fighters by having to challenge each other.

We are to fight the good fight for the true faith. We are to prepare ourselves by working hard to understand God's Word well,
by devoting ourselves to prayer and other spiritual training, and
by pursuing a godly life—a life that is marked by perseverance,
gentleness, and love.

When we fight for the faith with other believers, we challenge one
another to keep persevering and keep learning. We spur one another
on toward lives of humility and service. We encourage one another
to hold on tightly to the hope that we have—the hope of heaven.

And hopefully, no one will get knocked out in the process.

Lord, help me keep fighting the good fight. Amen. —M.L.

Even Demons Shudder

*You believe that there is one God. Good!
Even the demons believe that—and shudder.*
JAMES 2:19

No one really wants to be compared to a demon. But that doesn't stop James. He tells his listeners that faith without deeds is "useless" (v. 20). "A person is considered righteous by what they do and not by faith alone" (v. 24).

Works won't get a person into heaven, but true faith in Christ results in action too. God wants us to move. The Bible is full of verbs. Go. Tell. Baptize. Teach. Make. Do. Pray. Give. Serve. Love.

Saying we believe in God and yet doing nothing about that belief makes our faith ineffective. At least the demons have enough energy to shudder and enough sense to be frightened of the living God. When we are apathetic or lazy, we can actually even hurt God's kingdom by delivering a bad image of Christianity.

During natural disasters, the news follows the stories of those who are helping, doing, giving, and serving. No one wants to report on the guy who is just sitting there. Let's agree to be doers of God's Word, not just readers. Let's be action figures instead of china dolls.

*Almighty God, strengthen my faith so
I can do works that glorify You. Amen. —M.L.*

To the Next Generation

Even when I am old and gray, do not forsake me,
my God, till I declare your power to the next generation,
your mighty acts to all who are to come.

PSALM 71:18

How did you learn about Jesus? Did you see colorful Bible stories from birth? Did you move around little felt figures in a Sunday school classroom? When did God first make His entrance into your heart and mind?

Did you start reading a Bible on your own, or did someone read it to you? Did you learn through sermons or songs?

As we get older, we need to be grateful for those who have gone before us—those who committed time and energy to teaching us about God. And we need to think about what we're doing to help the next generation to continue in this tradition of faith.

What can we do to help bring Bible stories alive for kids? What can we do to tell our young neighbors about the hope of heaven?

It doesn't have to be complicated or high tech. It just needs to be real. And it needs to happen soon.

Lord, give me the words and confidence to teach others about
Your righteousness and faithfulness. You have been so good to
me—I want to make sure today's world knows. Amen. —M.L.

Redemption

*Coming up to them at that very moment, she gave
thanks to God and spoke about the child to all who were
looking forward to the redemption of Jerusalem.*
Luke 2:38

There she was, in her familiar corner. Out of the way of the foot traffic, but still easily seen if you knew where to look. Her head was almost always bowed, and her shoulders curved forward, bent and molded into place by her habitual posture of prayer.

Night and day, Anna stayed at the Temple. Watching. Waiting. Worshipping her God, her King. She loved the Lord more than she could ever put into words. For years upon years, she had spent every waking hour in conversation with her Creator. She was the picture of faithfulness.

On the day that the young couple brought the baby boy to be consecrated to the Lord, Anna was in her usual spot. A stir in the courtyard made her turn. There was old Simeon—taking a baby in his arms and praising God! Anna came close.

Simeon gently laid the child back into the mother's arms. Anna smiled at the girl, for the woman holding the babe was so young. Then she saw the face of the infant and she bowed down. "Thanks be to God!" From that day until her death, she never stopped speaking about the child who was to bring the redemption of Jerusalem. Her King!

*Lord, may my faithfulness be rewarded by
seeing the face of my King! Amen. —M.L.*

Walking with God

*Noah was a righteous man, blameless among the
people of his time, and he walked faithfully with God.*
GENESIS 6:9

"Walking with God" is a concept we find in the Bible that refers to people who had a close relationship with the Lord. Noah was one of these special people. In a world full of violence and evil behavior, God found that only Noah would obey Him.

But what about Noah's wife? Behind every strong man of God there is often some woman—a sister, mother, spouse, friend—supporting him and encouraging him and helping him stay on the right path. We don't hear much about Noah's wife, but God thought enough of Noah's family that He wanted to spare their lives, and start the new world with them.

For every step of Noah's obedient way, his wife was right there with him. All those days and weeks when he was gathering supplies and tools and, well, *lots* of animals, Noah's wife was right there with him. She didn't stop him. There are no reports of her complaining. She just kept going, and she kept him going too.

When a man or woman in this world is trying to walk with God, it is a good thing to have a partner walking right alongside them.

*Lord God, help me to always walk with You. And show
me how to help others walk with You too. Amen. —M.L.*

Blot It Out

Have mercy on me, O God, according to your unfailing love;
according to your great compassion blot out my transgressions.
PSALM 51:1

Wouldn't it be lovely to start life over with an absolutely shining, brand-sparkling-new, clean slate? Or maybe you would just like to erase certain sections of your life—maybe even just certain hours of certain days.

If you had the chance to clean up your record—to get rid of the sins you have committed—what parts would you want to delete? What if you could choose only one thing to get rid of?

We will never get that choice, sadly. We have to live with the consequences of the choices we make. Sometimes that means we have to live with the knowledge that we have hurt others. Sometimes we just have to deal with the internal battle of our souls. In any case, sin leaves a stain that we can never clear away on our own.

However, we have a great and gracious God, full of mercy and unfailing love. And He has made a way for us to come to Him with a clean and pure life. But we do have to come to Him first. We have to ask. And we need to mean it.

Have mercy on me, Lord. I have sinned before You.
I have sinned against You. Blot out my sins. Clean
up my record, Lord. Thank You. Amen. —M.L.

Thoughtful Believing

*The simple believe anything, but the
prudent give thought to their steps.*
PROVERBS 14:15

Many people, even churchgoing believers, often have the idea that to be a faithful follower of Christ you have to leave your brains at the door. That is, you can't really think too hard or look too closely at Christianity, or you will start to doubt. Or some believe that Christians are just blindly following a movement and not thinking it through.

But you can look closely at Christian history and think carefully about your own beliefs and ask good, hard questions. In fact, you should. God gave you a brain—it was one of His many gifts. Use it! The writer of Proverbs even urges us to get wisdom and get understanding.

It's extremely important—even life-changing—to be certain about what we believe and why we believe it. First, it will help us distinguish between what is a true principle and what is false. But also it will enable us to explain it to others in a compelling way.

So go ahead, bring your brains. Be thoughtful. Ask questions. God has all the best answers.

*Dear Lord, help me to remember to come to
You first with all my tough questions. Then help
me understand the answers. Amen.* —M.L.

What's in Store

I have fought the good fight, I have finished the race,
I have kept the faith. Now there is in store for me the crown
of righteousness, which the Lord, the righteous Judge,
will award to me on that day—and not only to me, but
also to all who have longed for his appearing.
2 TIMOTHY 4:7–8

Do you have a bucket list? What things do you want to accomplish before you are unable to accomplish much at all? Have you ever thought about what you'd like people to say about you at the end of your life? What do you want God to say about you?

Paul was confident in his standing before God. He knew he had tried as hard as he could to do what God had asked him to do. And he writes about this—not as a boast, but as an encouragement to the others "who have longed for his appearing."

Living a life of faith is not easy. It requires fighting against temptations, desires, and situations. It requires running hard toward the way of truth, goodness, and mercy. But at the end of the race, there is no better prize than the crown of righteousness—awarded by our Lord, the Judge.

Oh, Lord, my Judge, help me to be found
worthy of Your award. Amen. —M.L.

Nonperishable

Praise be to the God and Father of our Lord Jesus Christ!
In his great mercy he has given us new birth into a living hope
through the resurrection of Jesus Christ from the dead, and
into an inheritance that can never perish, spoil, or fade.

1 Peter 1:3–4

People often like to give fragile or expensive gifts to babies that the child may never touch—beautifully painted, porcelain piggy banks or solid silver spoons. Some people just give money, or perhaps deposit a donation to the child's college fund. Some newborns have enough money in their bank accounts to buy their own presents, go to college, and even purchase a new car.

We are the children of God. And though we have been born into a broken world, we have also been born into a living hope. Even the most precious baby gifts will eventually perish, spoil, or fade. The piggy bank will crack or the spoons will tarnish. The monetary gifts will someday be spent. But our inheritance—our place in the kingdom of God—will always be ready for us.

Thank You, Lord, for living and dying and rising again—all for us!
I'm so excited to know that I am an heir of Your kingdom—
that someday I will get to see Your face. Amen. —M.L.

In a Flash

*For the Son of Man in his day will be like the lightning, which
flashes and lights up the sky from one end to the other.*
LUKE 17:24

The night air holds the heat of the day. Tree branches stand still
against the violet clouds of dusk. Far away, a low rumble announces
the coming thunderstorm.

As you watch, a flash of light appears and then bounces, seemingly flitting from cloud to cloud, until it disappears. You wait for a
minute, holding your breath. And the sky lights up again, showing
off streaks of pink that have been added to the scene. Again and
again the flashes come, as the rumbling gets louder.

Some people look to these same skies, asking God to open up
the heavens and show them the day when Jesus will come again.
They look for signs. But they should stop looking and start doing.

Jesus said His day, the day of His coming, will come like a flash—
with no warning of its appearance and a quickness that cannot be
recorded. He will come in an instant, lighting up our world once
again with His power and glory. Will you be ready?

*Jesus, my Lord, I look forward to the day when You will shine
again here. We need Your light. But until that day comes, help me
to remember to do all that You have told me to do. Amen. —M.L.*

God Knows My Grief

Be merciful to me, LORD, for I am in distress; my eyes grow weak with sorrow, my soul and body with grief.

PSALM 31:9

Grief is a lonely valley; a tiny boat on a vast, choppy sea; a hole in a cave in the depths of the earth.

Even when friends try to join you there, somehow they can't really break in. Grief can suck you in like a muddy swamp.

Grief makes it hard to look outside yourself, to see anything past your own sorrow.

But God knows our grief. He shaped our hearts. He knows what things bring us sorrow. He knows how long our hearts can ache.

Grief hurts. But even when we feel as though our world will never be whole again, it's good to remember that God is there with us. And we can cry out to Him. We can complain to Him. We can rage at Him. We can sob in front of Him. And He will still be there. And He will grieve with us.

Father God, I know You know my heart. I don't want to be sad forever, Lord. Please soften this pain. Please heal my ache. Please restore my soul. Please let me smile again. Amen. —M.L.

Energy

*He is the one we proclaim, admonishing and teaching
everyone with all wisdom, so that we may present everyone
fully mature in Christ. To this end I strenuously contend
with all the energy Christ so powerfully works in me.*
COLOSSIANS 1:28–29

Proclaiming, admonishing, teaching. Everyone! Everyone? Really? With all wisdom. . .what wisdom?

All of this sounds like so much to do. How are we supposed to teach others about Him when we feel like we can hardly grasp who He is? How are we to present everyone as fully mature when we can't even get people to show up on time?

But bit by bit, it can be done. We can challenge one another. We can educate one another. We can point things out to one another that need to be changed or mended or corrected.

And we don't have to do it alone. In fact, we probably can't. All the energy we need for this task is supplied by Christ. He is the one who allows us to keep going when we are weary of dealing with one another. He is the one who urges us to keep going when the fight in front of us seems too difficult. He is our friendly fuel.

*Dear Jesus, thank You for supplying everything I need to
live out Your purpose for me. Thank You for giving me
energy I so desperately crave. Amen. —M.L.*

Everlasting

Do you not know? Have you not heard? The LORD is the everlasting God, the Creator of the ends of the earth. He will not grow tired or weary, and his understanding no one can fathom.

ISAIAH 40:28

He never tires.

He creates worlds. He gathers seas. He shapes mountains. And He never gets tired.

He blows the wind across the deserts. He pulls in the tides. He digs out trenches in the oceans. He places the stars in the sky. He forms creatures with intricate details and infinite variety. And He never is exhausted.

He shapes every human. He listens to every heart. He watches the gears in each mind. He breathes life into all of us and sets the world spinning. He tends our souls.

And He never gets weary.

Our God goes on and on, from before the beginning of time. He never stops. He never sleeps. He never forgets. He never ignores. He never, ever ends. And He loves us forever.

How does He do it? We cannot fathom the dimensions of a mind from which all this beauty, all this creativity, all this complexity, and all this energy come. There is no one like our God.

Lord, I get so weary sometimes. I'm so thankful that You never get tired of me. Amen. —M.L.

Like a Child

"I tell you the truth, anyone who doesn't receive the Kingdom of God like a child will never enter it."
LUKE 18:17 NLT

They love ice cream and laughter. They like to spin in circles, round and round, until they get so dizzy they fall on the ground. They love to be tickled. They cannot successfully tell a lie. They want to tell you everything. They want to be tagged. They want to run and run and run, to jump and be caught. They want to fly. They think rainbows are painted in the sky.

Children are beautiful gifts from God. And Jesus loved them, every one of them. And Jesus knew the thing that we grown-ups sometimes forget—that children believe. Children have faith. Children know and love Jesus in a simple, pure way that we all too quickly grow out of.

Jesus called the children to Him. He rebuked his disciples for trying to keep the children from Him. They weren't a bother! They were a blessing!

Living in the Kingdom of God—loving and accepting people, saying I'm sorry, letting others go first, sharing, being fair, showing mercy—these are all things that children learn quite easily or do quite naturally. These are all things we can learn from them.

*Lord, help me remember what it's like
to believe like a child. Amen. —M.L.*

Rich

Teach those who are rich in this world not to be proud and not to trust in their money, which is so unreliable.
1 TIMOTHY 6:17 NLT

Our small and large screens are filled with people who have more riches than they could possibly use. Professional sports players making millions for playing grown-up games, movie stars one-upping one another with the latest trends, even social media stars—challenging one another to rack up an ever-increasing sum of "likes."

Sometimes people earn money for nothing other than making fun of other people who are making money. It can all seem a bit ridiculous, especially when so many children still go to bed hungry every night.

But all this money is unreliable. These fortunes so easily gained can be easily spent in a flash. Lawsuits and medical crises and simply the changing whims of the viewing public can have a drastic effect on a star's income, sending someone from a mansion to a motel overnight.

We are meant to trust in something more substantial. Something that will not fade away.

Put your trust in God. Then you will be truly rich.

Lord, help me to value the right things. Help me never get caught up in monetary gain, but to use whatever resources I have to serve You. Amen. —M.L.

Citizens of Heaven

*Above all, you must live as citizens of heaven, conducting your-
selves in a manner worthy of the Good News about Christ. Then,
whether I come and see you again or only hear about you, I will
know that you are standing together with one spirit and one
purpose, fighting together for the faith, which is the Good News.*
PHILIPPIANS 1:27 NLT

Once we have accepted Jesus as our Savior, we keep learning about
what it means to obey the Lord. Much of what we learn will set us
apart from others. We may be seen as different because we like to
keep our wits about us instead of getting drunk. Or people may
wonder why we try to say kind things about even the most annoying,
insulting individuals. Or friends may wonder why we forgive people
who hurt us. Many people will scratch their heads and say, "Huh?
I don't get it."

But the more our actions reflect the character of Christ, the
easier it will be for us to tell the story of Christ—and have people
actually believe us. And the more we are able to tell the story of
Christ, the more united we become with other Christians all around
the world, all telling the same true story.

*Lord, help me to stay committed to
becoming more like You. Amen. —M.L.*

Such People

Such people claim they know God, but they deny him by the way they live. They are detestable and disobedient, worthless for doing anything good.

TITUS 1:16 NLT

Whenever anyone claims to know God, or when someone tries to draw attention to herself due to her supposedly great faith, a warning alarm should sound. *Alert! Alert! False claim ahead!*

We have to acknowledge that when we make our Christianity known, people will be watching us—considering our lives carefully as they try to figure out how we live differently from anyone else. If people see nothing different about the way we treat one another, about how we love and forgive and serve and so on—then it may mean we are not living right.

Before we open our mouths to claim a relationship with God, we should make sure our hands and feet are showing what living in the kingdom of God is like. We should evaluate ourselves and get rid of anything that could possibly fall in the "detestable and disobedient" category. We need to make sure that every part of who we are is worthy of doing good.

God of heaven, King of my kingdom, please forgive me if I've ever disappointed You by not showing others what You are truly like. Please help me be worthy of the work of declaring Your Gospel. Amen. —M.L.

We Don't Have to Get It

*The LORD directs our steps, so why try to
understand everything along the way?*
PROVERBS 20:24 NLT

There are times in our lives when reading the instructions, or digesting the instructions in some way, is essential. Maybe you can guess how to put that children's bookshelf together, but installing your superexpensive, brand-new TV on the wall had better be done with extreme care.

Sometimes you have to read all the instructions before you start an activity. It's wise to read recipes all the way through before you begin to cook food.

And reading the instructions can save you a lot of time, or can even save you from having an accident!

But much about life is uncertain and unpredictable. We don't always have instructions for every step. And even if we did, we wouldn't always have time to understand them.

Thankfully, we don't have to have every step of our journey figured out. God directs our steps. He leads us on the way. We don't have to understand all the whys and hows and wheres. We can follow Him, listen to Him, talk to Him, and learn from Him. And He will lead us to new heights of understanding every day.

*Lord, I'm so glad I don't have to understand every detail.
I'm so thankful my life is safe in Your hands. Amen. —M.L.*

Each Part

From him the whole body, joined and held together
by every supporting ligament, grows and builds
itself up in love, as each part does its work.
EPHESIANS 4:16

The human body is utterly astounding. Each system was designed to support the others. Each organ was formed and fit into the body in such a way as to maximize effectiveness. Each type of tissue was designed with a specific purpose. Each cell within that tissue was created to do a certain job.

There are no useless parts of the body. There are some we don't understand as well as others. And there are some that have to be removed at times (for example, wisdom teeth). But in order for a body to function well and be healthy, every part has to be in good order.

In the body of believers, no person is without purpose. Everyone is needed, with his or her unique gifts and abilities, to support the others, and to maximize the work of the kingdom of God. We can't just choose to remove someone, any more than we could kick out our hormones or pluck out a kidney. Every person is needed for us all to grow together.

Lord, help me to value every person. Help me to treat Your
church like the family You want it to be. Amen. —M.L.

Narrow Roads

"Enter through the narrow gate. For wide is the gate and broad is the road that leads to destruction, and many enter through it. But small is the gate and narrow the road that leads to life, and only a few find it."
MATTHEW 7:13–15

If you like to travel, you will find that many narrow roads wind around the world. There are rambling roads in Scotland, hugged on both sides by ancient stone walls as they make their way through busy villages. There are mountain passes where the road gives way to sheer drop-offs on either side—with nothing but rocks to land on.

Broad highways look easier at first. Plot a course destination on your GPS and it is likely to give you a route that includes lots of main highways. It's the fastest way to go. But "fastest" is not always "best" in terms of the kingdom of God.

The road to Jesus is a narrow way, with lots of surprise turns, but it leads to eternal life. It is wide enough for at least one person to travel on it—one person carrying a cross. Will you follow Him?

Jesus, I want to follow You wherever You go. Amen. —M.L.

All the People

*But they could think of nothing, because
all the people hung on every word he said.*
LUKE 19:48 NLT

After Jesus entered Jerusalem in a procession that drew quite a lot of attention—particularly from the unhappy Pharisees—His schedule was packed. He set about clearing the Temple of all the nonsacred business going on there. In an aggressive move, Jesus drove out the sellers.

Then He began teaching daily in the Temple. Of course, the religious leaders of the time did not like this at all. Once again, plans were put in place to kill the rabbi from Nazareth.

But once again, they couldn't do it. And why? What prevented them?

All the people.

All the people who came to hear Jesus speak.

All the people who came to be taught and to understand.

All the people who came to be healed.

All the people who came to worship.

There will come a time when the world's leaders once again try to get rid of Christ.

And who do you think needs to stop them?

All the people.

*Lord God, my leader and my teacher. Please help me to
understand Your will. Please teach me the right things
I need to do. Help me to be prepared to defend my
beliefs and to stand up for You. Amen. —M.L.*

Not to Us

Not to us, O LORD, not to us, but to your name give glory,
for the sake of your steadfast love and your faithfulness.
Why should the nations say, "Where is their God?"

PSALM 115:1–2 NRSV

Sometimes we get confused. We think we are focused on worshipping God, but we start worshipping worldly things instead. We start loving our music and the sound of our voices more than we love to sing the Lord's praise. We start loving our books about God's Word more than we love to read His Word alone. We start paying attention more to how we pray than we do to Who we are praying to.

We need to be careful not to set up new idols for ourselves. Especially when people are new to the faith, it can be easy to get the rituals and rites and traditions of the church muddled up with the purpose of the church.

We don't want the glory given to us and to our names. We don't need to be lifted up. We need to be crystal clear about the object of our adoration. And we need to shout His praise to all the nations.

O Lord, I want to praise You and You only. Help me to stay
clearly focused on You. Help me not get distracted with
things of the world. I will praise You now! Amen. —M.L.

Breath of Jesus

Again Jesus said, "Peace be with you! As the Father has sent me,
I am sending you." And with that he breathed on them and said,
"Receive the Holy Spirit. If you forgive anyone's sins, their sins are
forgiven; if you do not forgive them, they are not forgiven."
JOHN 20:21–23

What must the breath of Jesus feel like? Like the warmth of a thousand suns shining on green meadows. . .like the coolness of a spring breeze blowing through the trees. . .like the crisp, crackling air of the first autumn day. . .

What must the breath of Jesus smell like? Like the scent of a million wildflowers at the height of summer. . .like the salty, fresh bite of ocean air. . .like the delicious aroma of a rich blend of hot coffee. . .

What must the breath of Jesus do? Maybe it refreshes your mind like cold mountain water from a brook by your campsite. . . . Maybe it soothes your aches like a healing, natural balm. . . . Maybe it wraps you up in a thick blanket of warmth and soft goodness.

What an amazing way to be sent out into the world!

Lord Jesus, You are so amazing to me.
Breathe on me, Jesus. Refresh my spirit. Amen. —M.L.

He Will Dwell with Us

And I heard a loud voice from the throne saying, "See, the home of God is among mortals. He will dwell with them; they will be his peoples, and God himself will be with them; he will wipe every tear from their eyes. Death will be no more; mourning and crying and pain will be no more, for the first things have passed away."

REVELATION 21:3–4 NRSV

Sometimes when this world has become rather gray and cold and the news stories are especially grim, it is good to think on the hope we have in God.

He knows our troubles. He knows what is tearing our world apart. And He is in control of it all. He has a plan for us. He has a plan to bring everyone into the light of His kingdom. He doesn't want to leave anyone behind.

And then one day we will join Him in that city where there is no death and darkness, no sorrow and suffering. And He will be our God and we will forever be His people. The home of God will be right here!

Lord God, I can't wait till the day that I get to live with You! Thank You for this promise and this hope in which we live. Amen. —M.L.

No Fading

Only be careful, and watch yourselves closely so that you do not forget the things your eyes have seen or let them fade from your heart as long as you live.

DEUTERONOMY 4:9

The girl squinted her eyes at the wall where she had been peeling away layer after layer of wallpaper. Something was written under this layer. It was in a small script, and with tiny, beautiful lettering. She carefully peeled back a bit more of the crumbling paper and focused on the script. "For God. . .so loved the world. . ." The familiar words of John 3:16 spread out on the wall, then disappeared beneath another layer of paper.

Who must have written that there, and how long ago? It must have been fifty or sixty years ago, by the look of the paper. The lettering was lovely, but neat and careful like a child's handwriting. Maybe this was a child's way of remembering her Bible verse. Or maybe it was her favorite one.

Though we may not write our verses on the wall, we should take care to remember God's Word. To hide it in our hearts. To memorize as much of it as we can. His Word will get us through many difficult days. And its power never fades.

Lord, thank You for sweet reminders
of Your Word. Amen. —M.L.

Unseen Footprints

Your path led through the sea, your way through the mighty waters, though your footprints were not seen.

PSALM 77:19

This psalmist writes about a time when he was having trouble feeling God's presence. He doubted whether God was there for him. But instead of falling into confusion or anger over his situation (and God's seeming neglect), the writer remembers all the things God has done for him and for His people in the past.

We would do well if we took this writer's experience as an example. At times when life is hard and we don't understand where to find God, it's often easiest for us to see Him in places He has already been. Once we start considering all that God has done for us personally—all the blessings He has given us—and start listing all the wonders He has created for the world, we will find that He is very much with us now, just as He has always been.

We can't always see His footprints walking with us through this life and leading us along the way, but we can be sure He is always there.

Lord, thank You for leading me. Thank You for being there for me, even at times when I can't see or feel that You are there. Amen. —M.L.

Everywhere

The Lord's message rang out from you not only in Macedonia and Achaia—your faith in God has become known everywhere.

1 Thessalonians 1:8

The church at Thessalonica had put themselves on the map—the faith map. Reports had gone out that they were followers of Christ. They had become a model to believers in the region. They had turned away from idols to worship the one true God.

Wouldn't it be amazing if every church was known for its commitment to Jesus? If, instead of having a reputation for gossip, or divisions, or scandals, the Christian church was simply known as the best place to go to see Jesus in action?

What can you do today, in your community, in your church, to make your faith in God known everywhere? What can you do to serve others in humility? What can you do to love others unconditionally? What can you do to give to someone generously?

The Thessalonians certainly were not perfect. But they were dedicated to making Jesus' name known—everywhere.

Lord Jesus, I want people to know that I know You.
I want my life to reflect the story of Your Gospel.
Please get rid of things in my life that are hindering
my efforts to show others Your love. Amen. —M.L.

Hidden Life

Set your minds on things above, not on earthly things.
For you died, and your life is now hidden with Christ in God.
COLOSSIANS 3:2–3

Paul tells us to set our minds on things above—not things below. And just in case you are wondering what the "things below" are, he gave us a list of examples of things of the earthly nature (vv. 5, 8). These include sexual immorality of various sorts, evil desires, greed, anger, and foul language.

Now, no one said it would be easy to get these things out of your mind and out of your life. You'll have to take deliberate steps to avoid certain temptations. You might need to go different places, change your routines, or even hang out with different people for a while, until you are strong enough to stay focused on godly things. You will also need to fill your mind with God's Word, with prayer, with praise, and with wise words from godly counselors.

Consider what would happen if you had physically died—you would be disconnected from every worldly thing you used to know. That is how God wants you to live—disconnected from the worldly desires, and wholly plugged in to Him.

Lord, help me to avoid the temptations that strike my weakest points. Please give me the strength to live for You. Amen. —M.L.

Good Judgment

David said to Abigail, "Praise be to the L<small>ORD</small>, the God of Israel, who has sent you today to meet me. May you be blessed for your good judgment and for keeping me from bloodshed this day and from avenging myself with my own hands."
1 S<small>AMUEL</small> 25:32–33

Being a woman of faith doesn't just mean thinking about following God. Sometimes (most of the time) it means getting up and doing what needs to be done, right then and there. It means jumping into action, whatever action is required.

Our actions may not stop a battle, but we could stop a battle of words. We might not be able to bring peace, but we could help two sides to see each other's stories. We might not be able to stop someone from making a wrong choice, but we could present some other options.

How do we prepare to be people who can make good judgments quickly? Ask God. Go to His Word and see the examples of people who lived wisely. Most of all, study who Jesus was and is and is to come.

Lord, I want to be like Abigail—I want to be able to think quickly on my feet and use sound judgment. I want to be a peace-bringer. Will You help me, please? Amen. —M.L.

Best Teaching Practices

*Anyone who runs ahead and does not continue in the
teaching of Christ does not have God; whoever continues
in the teaching has both the Father and the Son.*

2 John 9

Maybe you are just starting to learn about the Christian faith. You're not a Bible scholar and you haven't been in church all your life. So you may be wondering, *How am I to know what teaching is from God and what isn't?*

First of all, realize you are not alone in asking this question. Even people who have been walking in the faith for some time have difficulties at times understanding who is a good teacher to follow and who isn't.

So what can you do? Spend time in God's Word on your own. Read it. Memorize it. Read it again. There are many good Bible study tools that will help you get the most out of your time with the Bible. Ask a pastor or a friend to help you find some helpful resources.

Then listen carefully to what a teacher says. If the teacher is not referring often to God's Word, or if the teacher is asking you to follow something you know to be contrary to God's Word, then it may be time to find a new teacher.

*Lord, help me to discern the wisdom
that comes from You. Amen. —M.L.*

Encourage Your Heart

*May our Lord Jesus Christ himself and God our Father,
who loved us and by his grace gave us eternal
encouragement and good hope, encourage your hearts
and strengthen you in every good deed and word.*

2 THESSALONIANS 2:16–17

We live in a fast-paced time, and it's affected the way we speak to one another. Not many people write long, old-fashioned letters anymore. Not many people even bother to communicate on a regular basis with whole sentences. Sometimes our messages to each other are more filled with images than they are with letters.

And that's not all bad. This is not a rant about returning to the old days and getting rid of our cellphones. But we are missing out on vital, vibrant aspects of communication when we don't take time to speak to one another in complete thoughts—or even go really old school and meet face-to-face.

To encourage someone and strengthen a person, you have to know that person's fears and weaknesses. You have to know where they need support. The best way to find that out is to sit with them, talk with them, and work alongside them. Who are you in a relationship with that you could help encourage and strengthen?

*Lord, You are such an encouragement to me. Every time
I need a boost, You are there to show me where I've done
well. Help me provide that kind of encouragement
to someone today. Amen.* —M.L.

Not Used Up

So there was food every day for Elijah
and for the woman and her family.
1 KINGS 17:15

The dog is sick. The kids forgot their homework. The bus is late. The dinner is cold. The work is too much. The family is too much. Everything is too much.

You feel used up. You're only one person—how can you possibly do it all?

God wants to remind you that you don't have to.

Elijah went to Zarephath during a drought, and everyone's supplies were running low. God told Elijah to go ask a widow for provisions. So he did. But the widow wanted to be clear, "I don't have any bread—only a handful of flour in a jar and a little olive oil in a jug. I am gathering a few sticks to take home and make a meal for myself and my son, that we may eat it—and die."

This was a woman who felt all used up. She was in a desperate situation. And now here's one more person who wants something from her. But Elijah told her that God had made a promise: "The jar of flour will not be used up and the jug of oil will not run dry until the day the LORD sends rain on the land" (1 Kings 17:14). And God was true to His Word. And the woman was filled.

Fill me up too, Lord! Amen. —M.L.

Keeper of the Deep

*He gathers the waters of the sea into jars; he puts the
deep into storehouses. Let all the earth fear the Lord;
let all the people of the world revere him.*

Psalm 33:7–8

Imagine the largeness, the hugeness, the utter enormity of our great God! He can pour an ocean into a jar. He can gather the deep into storage, and save it for another day.

Anyone who is that big and that powerful is someone to be feared. He is someone to be respected. But our Lord is also someone to be loved. And He loves us with all the depth and width and height and length of His giant heart.

We cannot conceive of the measure of our Lord. We cannot fathom someone of such greatness. But we don't have to. We can feel the magnitude of His love—a love that goes further than we can ever imagine. A love big enough to conquer death. A love generous enough to forgive a lifetime of sins. A love strong enough to hold us all.

*Lord, You are so great and so, so good. I don't understand
You, but I want to know You more. I want to be held in Your
huge hands and protected by Your awesome love. Teach me
to respect You. Show me how to love You. Amen. —M.L.*

Rejoicing Together

*Her neighbors and relatives heard that the Lord
had shown her great mercy, and they shared her joy.*
LUKE 1:58

The priest Zechariah and his wife, Elizabeth, were descendants of Aaron. Zechariah and Elizabeth had prayed and prayed for a child, but still none came. But when Zechariah went in to serve at the Temple, an angel surprised him with astonishing news—he was going to have a son! The angel of the Lord said, "He will be a joy and delight to you, and many will rejoice because of his birth, for he will be great in the sight of the Lord" (vv. 14–15). The same angel, Gabriel, visited the young Mary—Elizabeth's relative. The angel informed the shocked Mary that she was to give birth to the Son of God, and that Elizabeth, in her old age, was pregnant too. "For no word from God will ever fail" (v. 37).

When Elizabeth gave birth to her son, whom they named John, everyone around her praised God. And Zechariah, who hadn't been able to speak during Elizabeth's pregnancy (due to his doubt of the angel's message), was suddenly filled with the Holy Spirit and praised God in song. And all the neighbors were filled with awe when they heard about this story, and they praised God as well.

People love to celebrate the birth of babies. How much more so when the baby is a true miracle of God!

Lord, thank You for birthing miracles! Amen. —M.L.

True Value

Kings take pleasure in honest lips;
they value the one who speaks what is right.
PROVERBS 16:13

Every king (or queen) needs some trustworthy person to count on—someone to give him (or her) advice and guidance. Many people flatter and praise a leader's actions, but they have ulterior motives. They want to get honor and power for themselves. Or they want to shape the leader's plans so that they will reap some benefits.

The king needs a person who is selfless—who speaks the truth, even when it's difficult or unpleasant. Leaders need men and women with servant hearts—able to contribute to the leadership by serving in humility.

What kind of adviser would you be? Would you be able to take the challenge of speaking the truth to power? Or would you cave in and join the flattery club? Would you try to grab power for yourself? What kind of friend are you? Are you faithful and true in speech and action? Or do you twist the truth to make people feel better?

Dear Lord, help me to keep honest lips, whether I'm speaking
to royalty or just to my good friend. Guard my tongue in all
situations, so I can speak what is right. Amen. —M.L.

Foreigners

*Dear friends, I urge you, as foreigners and exiles, to abstain
from sinful desires, which wage war against your soul.
Live such good lives among the pagans that, though they
accuse you of doing wrong, they may see your good
deeds and glorify God on the day he visits us.*
1 Peter 2:11–12

Have you ever traveled to a country or a region where not many people spoke your native tongue? It's bewildering. You hear conversations all around you, but none of them make sense. You strain for understanding. You exhaust yourself with listening hard to every sentence trying to discover meaning. Nothing looks, feels, or smells familiar.

Now consider living as a Christian in today's world. Are you ever that exhausted? Or do you feel completely fine, because you fit in so well, no one can tell how your life is different from anyone else's.

When Peter encouraged his friends to live differently, he didn't necessarily want them to be frustrated. But he didn't want them to blend right in either. God wants us to live lives that reflect Jesus Christ—and if we do that, people are going to notice.

*Lord, help me to stand out from others in all the best
ways. Remind me not to take pride in anything I do,
but to always give You the glory. Amen. —M.L.*

All She Had

*But a poor widow came and put in two very
small copper coins, worth only a few cents.*
MARK 12:42

What do you have to give? Perhaps you are doing very well finan-
cially, and enjoy giving generously from your plenty. But what if you
have very little? Maybe you're a single mom with three kids, just
trying to make ends meet. And maybe the ends just never meet.

God wants us to give with a cheerful heart. And some days,
that is pretty hard to do if your bank account is slim and your kids
are hungry. It's agonizing to put your trust in God when you feel it's
your duty to make everything right. But God has been providing
for you all along, and He's not going to stop now.

But if you give what you can, knowing you are showing honor
and gratitude to God, God will bless your efforts.

As Jesus watched the rich and poor bringing their offerings to
the Temple, He said to His disciples, "Truly I tell you, this poor widow
has put more into the treasury than all the others. They all gave out
of their wealth; but she, out of her poverty, put in everything—all
she had to live on" (Mark 12:43–44).

*Lord, help me to be generous with what I have.
Help me to trust You to provide all I need. Amen. —M.L.*

The God We Serve

What god will be able to rescue you from my hand?
DANIEL 3:15

At some point in our lives, in our walk with Christ, our faith will be put to the test. It may be a trial that involves our family. It may be a sickness. It may be a financial struggle. It may be an accident that causes severe injuries.

We have no way of knowing when disaster will strike us. But at some point, every person will be tested. Some of us may be tested many times.

Shadrach, Meshach, and Abednego were tested in an extreme way. Because they would not worship an idol, King Nebuchadnezzar had them thrown into the blazing furnace. But before he punished them, he gave them one more chance—a chance to escape certain death. He said if they would serve his gods, he would let them go. And then he asked them, if they were thrown into the furnace instead, who would be able to rescue them?

The three friends had a courageous and honest answer: "If we are thrown into the blazing furnace, the God we serve is able to deliver us from it. . . . But even if he does not, we want you to know, Your Majesty, that we will not serve your gods or worship the image of gold you have set up" (Daniel 3:17–18).

And that is the God we serve. The kind of God who can give us fiery courage in the face of flames of destruction.

Dear Lord, help me to have some of
that fiery courage today! Amen. —M.L.

Disputed

*Is it possible that there is nobody among you wise
enough to judge a dispute between believers?*
1 Corinthians 6:5

Churches split over the most ridiculous things: carpet color, chair choice, worship style, pastor's salary, someone-said-something-about-someone-else, to-VBS-or-not-to-VBS, and so on. The list of so-called reasons for tearing a family of believers apart is too long by a mile.

Why is it that we just cannot settle our disputes ourselves? Why do we so quickly get to the point of taking someone to court or raising a complaint with a church board? Why is it so hard for people to sit down together, present arguments, and come to a compromise?

Certainly, we don't see this happening on a large scale among our government leaders. Perhaps we just aren't being taught how to argue anymore. Maybe we all need more education in this area. Maybe debate clubs need to exist not just for kids, but for grown-ups. Maybe we need to see some disputes worked out in a public forum, so each side is held accountable to what they say and how they treat one another. And maybe we all need more patience.

*Lord, I know our petty arguments must grieve You. The way
we treat each other at times is so rude and uncaring. It is not
the way You meant Your creations to act. Please forgive us.
Please help us to do better. Amen. —M.L.*

I Am

*"You aren't one of this man's disciples too, are you?"
she asked Peter. He replied, "I am not."*
JOHN 18:17

Just three little words. But so much deception.

Just three little words. But so much betrayal.

Just three little words. But so much fear.

Peter must have been extremely confused and disheartened as he followed Jesus to the high priest's courtyard on the night that Jesus was betrayed. Here was the man who was supposed to be his King—being led away by guards. *What will Jesus do?* Peter must have wondered. Perhaps he hadn't quite given up hope just yet, but he had given up courage.

Presented with a straightforward chance to pledge his faithfulness to his Lord, Peter failed. Then he failed again. And again. And with each failure, no doubt his confidence in himself and in his friend Jesus' ability to forgive him probably dwindled a little too.

One wonders if Peter had the chance to do those scenes of his betrayals over again, would he still say those three little words? Or would he just say two? What would you say if you had been in his sandals? What do you say now? "Are you a disciple?"

"I am."

Lord, I've let You down before. Sometimes I've even pretended I didn't love You. And sometimes I've tried to hide from You. Please forgive me, Lord. Amen. —M.L.

Known Inside and Out

You have searched me, LORD, and you know me. You know when I sit and when I rise; you perceive my thoughts from afar. You discern my going out and my lying down; you are familiar with all my ways.

PSALM 139:1–3

The old woman watched the young couple for many months. She would sit on her porch for most of the day, and just watch. She watched the car go out, and she watched it come back in. She knew about what time they each got home from work, and she knew when they left in the morning.

Sometimes they ate breakfast on their front porch. She could see the particular treats they liked. She knew they liked coffee. Lots of it.

The old woman always hoped the couple would come say hello, but they never did. She longed to go say hello to them, but her legs were too frail to get her across the street.

So she just watched. And many days, she prayed for them.

God knows our goings-out and comings-in. God knows what's going on with us every single day. Better than a watchful neighbor, God even knows our thoughts. And He loves us still.

Maybe it's time we walked across the street and said hello to Him too.

Lord, I cannot even imagine why You are so interested in me. But I love that. And I love You. Amen. —M.L.

Hoping All Day Long

Guide me in your truth and teach me, for you are God my Savior, and my hope is in you all day long.

Beep! It's 6:45 a.m. The alarm goes off, and the busy day (just like every day) begins. There are kids to feed, clothes to fold, and dishes to put away. Then there's work at the office and work at the home and work in the middle. Then there's groceries to buy and bills to pay and food to cook. Then spend a little family time, then a little time for exercise, and everyone is off to bed.

Where did the day go? What did you accomplish today? Do you even know? And where was God in your day?

If you are going to follow Jesus, you need to make time for Him in your schedule. It may not be easy at first, but it is necessary. You can carve out some time in the morning for some prayer, take fifteen minutes at lunch to meditate on His Word, and take some time in the evening to pray with your kids. It doesn't have to be complicated or superstructured.

But place your hope in God, not in your busy schedule, all day long.

Lord, from the time I wake in the morning, until I go to bed at night, let me trust in You. Amen. —M.L.

Wholeheartedly

*"No one from this evil generation shall see the good land I swore to give your ancestors, except Caleb son of Jephunneh. He will see it, and I will give him and his descendan*ts *the land he set his feet on, because he followed the L*ORD *wholeheartedly."*
DEUTERONOMY 1:35–36

If you want to make a whole lot of difference in the world, you can't do it halfheartedly.

God was fed up with the Israelites, and you could see why. Time after time He had shown them how He was with them and would not leave them. Time after time He asked them to do something, and He was met by fear and complaints and negotiations. Those Israelites, former slaves that they were, just seemed to be imprisoned by the bonds of fear and punishment. They couldn't get over the idea that God was blessing them with a land, and that He would make sure they filled it. They just were too afraid to take the gift God was giving them.

Sometimes we're like that too, aren't we? We pray and pray and pray for something we want, some safety, some blessing, some good reward. And then when it gets handed to us, we try to figure it out, we overanalyze, and we miss out—because we're just too afraid of the challenge and opportunity.

Don't miss out. Have the courage of Caleb. Trust God's promises! He is faithful!

Lord, help me to accept the blessings You give
me with no fear or reservation. Amen. —M.L.

Get On with It

Do you see what this means—all these pioneers who blazed the way, all these veterans cheering us on? It means we'd better get on with it. Strip down, start running—and never quit! No extra spiritual fat, no parasitic sins. Keep your eyes on Jesus, who both began and finished this race we're in. Study how he did it.

HEBREWS 12:1–2 MSG

Hebrews 11 lists a great "cloud of witnesses." These were men and women of faith who showed great integrity and courage in their lives. They cut out a path we can all study and walk in—learning from their examples.

The writer of Hebrews then breaks into one of the best pep talks for living as a follower of Jesus. He says, all these have gone before us, and they're still supporting us! And then there's Jesus—and all that He sacrificed for us. If Jesus can carry a cross up a hill to endure horrible torture and scornful shame, then surely we can keep going.

Who are the pioneers that you look to as examples of great faith? It could be a well-known author or speaker, or a pastor you knew in your childhood, or a Sunday school teacher. No matter who that person is, think about why you consider them someone of great faith. And then, if you have the opportunity, thank them today!

Thank You, Lord, for great examples of faith! Amen. —M.L.

Saving Grace

*For the grace of God has app___ed
that offers salvation to all people.*
TITUS 2:11

How would you describe the gift of grace to someone who has never heard about it before?

It's like taking someone's ice cream, and then having them turn around and buy you a triple scoop—no strings attached.

It's like hitting your brother and then having him give you a kiss instead of a smack upside the head.

It's like taking someone's parking space, and then finding them washing your car later in the day. Just to be kind.

Grace is kind of like these situations, but it is so much more. Here's how Paul describes the grace of God: "It teaches us to say 'No' to ungodliness and worldly passions, and to live self-controlled, upright and godly lives in this present age, while we wait for the blessed hope—the appearing of the glory of our great God and Savior, Jesus Christ, who gave himself for us to redeem us from all wickedness and to purify for himself a people that are his very own, eager to do what is good" (vv. 12–14).

*God, thank You for this precious gift of
grace and call to grace. Amen. —M.L.*

The Queen of Hearts

She pleased him and won his favor.
ESTHER 2:9

When Esther (known also as Hadassah) was taken into the king's court as one of the candidates for queen, she was a young, simple Jewish woman. But she used her beauty and her simplicity and humility to gain the king's favor. And each step of the way, she, along with guidance from Mordecai, her adoptive father, looked for opportunities to gain more of a foothold in the king's heart. She so endeared herself to the king, that he wanted to do anything for her.

And when the time came for her to make the biggest request of her life, she was the only one who had any real chance of saving her people. Even though she risked her very life, it was her time to make a difference and save her people.

You may not have a nation to save, but there will be times in your life when you have opportunities available that could allow you to make a positive impact on others. Ask God to help you to be wise in your decisions and to keep your eyes open to take those chances when they come.

Lord, help me to be clever and brave like Esther. Help me to see places in my life where I can make a difference. Help me to see the benefits of my position that I can use to help others. Amen. —M.L.

Obey from the Heart

*But thanks be to God that, though you used to be slaves
to sin, you have come to obey from your heart the pattern
of teaching that has now claimed your allegiance.*

Romans 6:17

The little boy kicks his shoes off and one goes flying down the hallway and right through the pane of glass in the front door. This is the fourth pane of glass he has broken in that door. His mother pleads with him, "Why do you keep doing that when I tell you not to?" But all she gets in reply is a shrug of the shoulders.

We sometimes get stuck in a habit of doing the wrong things, and then we have trouble getting out of that rut. Only when we make a real heart change does outward change occur as well.

But once the mother told her son that she was sad because he had broken so many windows that they couldn't buy the special train that the boy wanted for his birthday, he understood the problem he was causing on a different level. And he stopped kicking off those big shoes.

Now, he might break something else, but we'll take the small victories.

*Lord God, help me to examine my patterns of behavior and
see if there are changes that I need to make. Amen. —M.L.*

Who Indeed?

Who has measured the waters in the hollow of his hand,
or with the breadth of his hand marked off the heavens?
Who has held the dust of the earth in a basket, or weighed
the mountains on the scales and the hills in a balance?
ISAIAH 40:12

Wars have been fought over one simple question: Whose god is better?

But when we consider the wonders of our Lord, when we consider the amazing design of His creation, it's hard to imagine how any god could compare. He is the God who made the striped zebra and the spotted cheetah. He is the God who formed us in His image and made us male and female. He is the omnipresent, omniscient, omnipotent God on high, who brought Himself down as low as He could go to be laid in a manger, just to show us His love.

No one but God claims this beautiful, personal relationship with His creation. No one but God claims to have conquered death, and has shown it in the bodily Resurrection. No one but God has a book of scripture that has largely remained intact for thousands of years and is respected by believers and nonbelievers alike.

Isaiah asks, "With whom, then, will you compare God?" (v. 18). Yes, who indeed?

Lord God, I stand in awe of You! Amen. —M.L.

Message Dwelling

Let the message of Christ dwell among you richly as you teach and admonish one another with all wisdom through psalms, hymns, and songs from the Spirit, singing to God with gratitude in your hearts.
COLOSSIANS 3:16

When you study the Word of God, you will find that it becomes a part of your worldview, but it also becomes a part of your language. It comes out in the way you speak to others. It can give you courage to point out the truth where so many falsehoods reside. It can give you a voice of praise, that you long to raise in worship to God. It can give you a voice of praise that you use to point out the good things your neighbor is doing.

It can compel you to talk to people you wouldn't normally talk to. It can convince you to forgive others, before you even realized you were holding a grudge. It can point out flaws in your own character that you never would have seen otherwise.

Let the Word of God, the message of Christ, the love of God the Father, God the Son, and God the Holy Spirit live in you and among you and inside your hearts.

Lord in heaven, bring Your message from heaven down to us. Let us hear it every day. Amen. —M.L.

While Waiting

*Wait for the LORD; be strong and
take heart and wait for the LORD.*
PSALM 27:14

Waiting. It can be pleasant and exciting. A bride waits with happy butterflies in her stomach, ready for the church doors to open and her father to lead her down the aisle.

It can be agonizing. The mother of the son who just overdosed waits in the hospital lobby to hear if the doctors were able to save him.

It can be confusing. The young woman sits outside the career counseling office, looking over her résumé. What in the world does she want to do with her life?

It can be lonely. The silver-haired woman sits in her dusty living room, all dressed up for church, waiting for her son, the son who doesn't show up—just like many other Sundays.

We wait for so many things and for so many different reasons. But waiting for the Lord is one kind of waiting we have no choice about. We cannot hurry God along. We don't know His schedule. But we can control what we do while waiting. We can be faithful. We can keep learning about Him. We can be devoted in prayer. We can be humble, serving others. We can be hopeful, looking forward always to the day we will see His face.

*Lord, help me to be strong and consistent
as I wait for You. Amen. —M.L.*

Bitter Weeds

Work at getting along with each other and with God.
Otherwise you'll never get so much as a glimpse of God.
Make sure no one gets left out of God's generosity.
Keep a sharp eye out for weeds of bitter discontent.
HEBREWS 12:15 MSG

The ragged, hairy, ugly things rise up in the worst places. They climb out of the ground right next to the stems of the roses, as if they know, the closer they get to the pretty plants, the more chance they have of going undetected.

Weeds. They grow at every opportunity—whether there are floods or droughts. They grow in every possible place—in the crack of a sidewalk, in a thin layer of dust on a barn floor, or even in the best, most well-groomed flower beds.

Just like weeds, seeds of bitterness start growing before we even know they are there. We think we are over that small, unkind joke made at our expense. We think we've forgotten not being invited to the baby shower. We think we don't care whether anyone liked the dish we brought to the potluck. But we're not over it, we haven't forgotten, and we do care.

Don't let bitterness grow in the cracks of your beautiful heart. Find it, face it, and ask God to help you weed it out!

Dear Lord, please help me find the roots of bitterness
in my soul, and help me get rid of them! Amen. —M.L.

No Retreat

But we do not belong to those who shrink back and are destroyed, but to those who have faith and are saved.
HEBREWS 10:39

Women have a common enemy. This enemy tears away at our identities and burrows into our hearts and tells us lies. "You are such a mess—you're never going to get it right." "You are unwanted." "You are incompetent." "You won't ever be good enough."

We have all met this enemy. And the enemy is *us*.

But we who follow Jesus ought to know better. Whenever this enemy whispers these falsehoods, we need to remember what the writer of Hebrews said. We have confidence—we have the ability and the permission to enter the Most Holy Place. Our entry tickets were bought with the blood of Christ. His precious sacrifice allows us to draw near to God with full—that's right, not half, not maybe, not almost—assurance. We have a sure hope, and we need to hold on to that hope without swaying or swerving to the left or right—without getting distracted by the other voices in our heads, or by temptations and desires that promise so much and give us nothing.

We must support each other. Encourage each other. Tell each other, "Don't throw away your confidence! Don't shrink back! Don't retreat!"

Because we have faith. We are saved. And we can defeat our enemy.

Lord, help me remember my confidence
comes straight from You! Amen. —M.L.

The Outsiders

Be wise in the way you act toward outsiders;
make the most of every opportunity.

Colossians 4:5

If you've never met a stranger, make a new friend wherever you go, and find a way to strike up conversation with anyone, anywhere, then you probably have the gift of gab. And if so, you probably don't find it too difficult to talk to people about Jesus.

Not everyone has the gift of evangelism, but we all have the duty and the responsibility to be good ambassadors for Jesus and the kingdom of God. But what if you are shy? What if you have trouble talking to people you don't know? What if you just don't know what to say?

Paul gives us some helpful hints: "Devote yourselves to prayer, being watchful and thankful" (v. 2). Spend time regularly talking to God, telling Him about your fears, reading about His life in His Word, and being grateful for what He's done for you. If you do these things, then the story of Jesus and what it means to you will be naturally at the front of your mind. And the next time you're in the grocery store, or waiting in line at the movies, or just out in the park, you might find it a little bit easier to "make the most of every opportunity," and tell someone about Jesus.

Lord, help me to be a good representative
of Your kingdom. Amen. —M.L.

Fearlessly

Pray also for me, that whenever I speak, words may be given me so that I will fearlessly make known the mystery of the gospel, for which I am an ambassador in chains. Pray that I may declare it fearlessly, as I should.
EPHESIANS 6:19–20

Your tongue feels fuzzy, and about the size of a golf ball. Your throat is dry and there's a little tickle way in the back where no one can scratch it. Your palms start to sweat and you can't get a deep breath.

No, you're not having an allergic reaction. It's just talking—you've been doing it since you were a toddler. Why is it so hard now?

Maybe because the message is so important.

When you are about to talk with someone about salvation and the good news of Christ, the one thing to keep in mind is that this is a message of love. When you are speaking to someone about their potential for a life in Christ, you are giving them a gift of love, just as someone once gave that gift to you.

Lord, help me to be confident as I speak to people about their salvation. Help me be clear in my explanation, and compassionate as I listen to their stories. Amen. —M.L.

The Secret

I know how to live on almost nothing or with everything.
I have learned the secret of living in every situation, whether
it is with a full stomach or empty, with plenty or little. For I
can do everything through Christ, who gives me strength.
PHILIPPIANS 4:12–13 NLT

What does "nothing" and "everything" look like to you?

Have you lived in a mansion? Have you grown up in a five-bedroom house with a six-car garage? Have you ever had to scavenge for food or lean on the generosity of strangers?

There are other kinds of "nothing." Maybe you've been through a lonely time, when you didn't have a friend in the world. Maybe you've been sunk into a depression so deep, you couldn't see any light.

There are other kinds of "everything." Maybe you've had a fantastic, fulfilling job. Maybe you've been surrounded by loving family and friends.

The secret to surviving the "nothing" times and staying humble during the "everything" times is not really that much of a secret after all. We just need to remember that anything we do is because we have Christ, and He gives us strength—to survive, to grow, to learn, to change, and to be thankful through it all.

Provider of all, Lord, I honor You. I give praise to You.
Help me to be content, no matter what is going on. Amen. —M.L.

Confrontations

I have been crucified with Christ and I
no longer live, but Christ lives in me.
GALATIANS 2:20

Probably one of the hardest, or at least the most uncomfortable, things you may have to do as a Christian person is to confront another brother or sister in Christ. There will come times when you see someone struggling with some aspect of their faith, or engaging in false teaching, or getting sucked into old bad habits, and you will be faced with a choice: do something or do nothing?

If you are living in obedience to Christ, you'll have to do something. But you should never call another person out just to amplify your self-image or to benefit yourself. You must examine your motives. If your motives are pure, then the first thing you need to do is ask the question: What's up with you?

Paul had a moment like this in Antioch. Peter (Cephas) had been eating among the Gentiles. But when Jews came to visit, he drew back from his Gentile friends. Paul called him out on this hypocritical behavior and reminded him that they are justified by faith, not by following the law of the Jews. Jesus came so that all might have a chance to be saved—not just certain groups.

And if Christ lives in us, then we need to act like Christ. And that's why we also need to hold each other accountable.

Lord, give me justice and mercy to be like You. Amen. —M.L.

He Breaks the Bow

Come and see what the LORD has done, the desolations he has brought on the earth. He makes wars cease to the ends of the earth. He breaks the bow and shatters the spear; he burns the shields with fire. He says, "Be still, and know that I am God."

PSALM 46:8–10

We hear murmurings of battles and wars. And no doubt, it's scary and troubling. Some leaders of countries and clans would rather have destruction than any kind of peace. There are people who will stop at seemingly nothing just to make a name for themselves.

But Jesus is the name above all names and the creator of peace. And we cannot forget the awesome, earth-melting, continent-crumbling power of our almighty God. When the harsh words of human minds become too much for you to process, turn to the Word of God, and find in those verses the comfort of being a child of an all-powerful, all-knowing King.

He will make the wars come to an end. He will bring peace—if He has to break every weapon and melt them down to do it. He will have us "be still and know." He is our God.

Lord, I want so much to see peace come to our world.
Show me how I can be a part of Your plan to bring
Your people peace. Amen. —M.L.

Imitators

Dear friend, do not imitate what is evil but what is good. Anyone who does what is good is from God. Anyone who does what is evil has not seen God.

3 JOHN 11

You've seen her on TV. She always looks so put together. So in control. So cool. So you go buy the brand she sells, paint your nails the same color, and get a similar haircut. You come home and look at yourself in the mirror, and. . .well, do you feel any different?

Maybe. Maybe not. But one thing's for certain—imitating someone doesn't instantly turn you into some other kind of person. It can take a long time for that change to happen.

And that's just one very good reason to imitate goodness. If you copy good behaviors, practice thinking on good things, and try to be the best person you can be, over time you will become not just a copy of goodness, but a person who lives as one who is from God.

But the opposite is also true. If you copy bad behaviors, repeat foul language, spend time dwelling on wrong thinking, and try to be like those who choose to do evil, over time you will become not just a copy of evil, but a person who has forgotten who you were created to be.

Creator God, I want to see You. Help me be more like You this day. Amen. —M.L.

Helper of the Fatherless

*But you, God, see the trouble of the afflicted; you consider
their grief and take it in hand. The victims commit
themselves to you; you are the helper of the fatherless.*

PSALM 10:14

Many children around the world have been orphaned due to illness, accidents, natural disasters, drug addiction, and other reasons. It would take an army to feed and clothe and care for them all. We see a vast problem like this, and we become overwhelmed.

But God sees these troubles too. And He is not overwhelmed—He takes their situation in hand. God the Father can fill the holes and wounds in a child's heart like no one else can. But we have a duty to these children as well.

As the hands and feet of our Father God, we must not turn away from those who have nowhere else to go. Consider carefully what you can do to be part of a system of people who are providing care for orphans today. You could sponsor a child, donate funds for specific needs, mentor a child in your area, or even consider becoming a foster or adoptive parent.

Remember: nothing is too hard for God, and He is on your side!

*Dear Father God, help me to see how I can help
children who have no fathers or mothers. Amen. —M.L.*

Forget the Scoffers

*Do they actually think they can make something of
stones from a rubbish heap—and charred ones at that?*
NEHEMIAH 4:2 NLT

Whenever you try to do a right thing in this world, you must often be prepared for an attack. Sometimes the attack comes straight from the enemy. And sometimes it comes from other kinds of enemies. But people will want to drag you down. They will want to steal your joy in doing good. Why? Who knows? There can be all kinds of reasons. Maybe they feel threatened. Maybe they feel jealous. Maybe they are just angry about something completely unrelated, and you, oh lucky person, get to feel the heat of their fury anyway.

Nehemiah was committed to organizing his fellow Jews and rebuilding the wall of Jerusalem. He felt it was a mission God had called him to fulfill. But he had enemies—people who didn't want to see Jerusalem established. And people who didn't care for the Jews.

These men scoffed at Nehemiah's efforts and threatened to kill him. But they persevered and finished that wall. And Nehemiah reported: "When our enemies and the surrounding nations heard about it, they were frightened and humiliated. They realized this work had been done with the help of our God" (Nehemiah 6:16 NLT).

So, keep going. Keep restoring good in your world. Others will see your work and honor God.

*Dear Lord, help me to not listen to the words of scoffers,
but listen to Your call on my life instead. Amen. —M.L.*

Speak the Truth

*"These are the things you are to do: Speak the truth to each
other, and render true and sound judgment in your courts;
do not plot evil against each other, and do not love to
swear falsely. I hate all this," declares the LORD.*
ZECHARIAH 8:16–17

There are not that many instances in the Bible where we find out about something that God hates. So when the Bible does tell us about what the Lord hates, we ought to pay attention.

God hates lying. This is clear from this passage from Zechariah. And He especially hates us lying to one another.

But we do this all the time. We lie to cover up sins. We lie to make people jealous. We lie to cause strife among others. We retell stories when we don't know whether they were true to begin with— but it's fun to tell them, so why not? In our courts of law, truth is often manipulated to sway a jury in favor of one client over another. Even our world leaders lie to and about one another—plotting to see who can look the best on the world stage.

So how do we get over this lying dependency? It begins with one truth at a time. You can start today! Try being honest all day long. And if you mess up, start again tomorrow!

Lord, help me speak the truth! Amen. —M.L.

A Place to Stand

Therefore, since we have been justified through faith, we have peace with God through our Lord Jesus Christ, through whom we have gained access by faith into the grace in which we now stand.
ROMANS 5:1–2

Have you ever been given special access to an exclusive club, or maybe to a "staff only" area? Perhaps you were handed a secret key or a special ID tag. A few swipes or turns and you are in. And everyone else is out.

We have been given access to a special place—a place of grace. Grace is a location—it is a position God gives us before His throne. It is a seat of honor—at the feet of our King—and yet it is also a seat of humility—understanding that the only way we are given this access is through God's gracious favor. We don't do anything to deserve this place. And we can't do anything to lose it. The access card or key will not be taken from us, as long as we follow Him.

It's a special place—but it's a place open to all who seek the Lord.

Lord God, thank You for the gift I can never, ever repay. Thank You for giving me access to Your grace. Help me to live out my life in thankfulness to You. Amen. —M.L.

Infinite Value

Yes, everything else is worthless when compared with the infinite value of knowing Christ Jesus my Lord. For his sake I have discarded everything else, counting it all as garbage, so that I could gain Christ and become one with him.

PHILIPPIANS 3:8–9 NLT

Imagine if one day you saw your neighbor emptying the contents of her house out onto her front lawn. She's tossing out antique lamps, ornate chairs, and old books. "Out it all goes!" she exclaims, as she tosses a priceless ruby necklace into an open trash bag. When you ask her why she's throwing away all this stuff, she answers, "It's all garbage compared to knowing Christ Jesus!"

Now, Christ may be calling you to downsize your possessions, but that isn't what these verses are talking about. Paul was describing all his many accomplishments, which he previously had used to persecute others and to put himself above others. For him, all those things that used to mean so much to him are now nothing compared to his relationship with Jesus.

So what do you really need to get rid of? What's taking up a spot in your heart that Jesus needs to occupy? What do you take too much pride in? Consider those things—not your album collection and velvet couch—and think about what needs to be trimmed out of your life today.

Dear God, help me to see what "garbage"
I need to take out. Amen. —M.L.

Be Humble

Don't be selfish; don't try to impress others. Be humble,
thinking of others as better than yourselves. Don't look out
only for your own interests, but take an interest in others, too.
PHILIPPIANS 2:3–4 NLT

It seems like such a simple command: "Don't be selfish." We can do that, right? Just think of others first. Think of others first. Think of others. . . *Oh wait, I have a concert to go to today—I'll have to pick up that food for my sick neighbor later. Or maybe I can get someone else to do it.*

Think of others first. Think of. . . *Ooooh, that new show comes out tonight. Gotta remember to watch that. Oh yeah, I was going to call my mom. Well, I can do that tomorrow.*

Think of others first. Think of. . . *Oh brother, I hate paying all these bills. Maybe I can just pay this one late so I can use this money to go to the movies this week with my friends. This guy probably doesn't need his money right now anyway.*

Think of oth— *Hmm, looks like there's only one piece of birthday cake left. Yeah, so it wasn't my birthday. So what? This cake is going to get stale if no one eats it. I'll just take care of it.*

Think. . . *Wow, I have been meditating on God's Word a lot already today. Now what was it I was supposed to be thinking of?*

Lord God, I'm having a hard time thinking of others first.
Please help me get rid of my selfish heart! Amen. —M.L.

Shadows

These are a shadow of the things that were to come;
the reality, however, is found in Christ.
COLOSSIANS 2:17

We celebrate milestones in people's lives and in the life of the church. We have feasts and festivals together. We have birthday parties and anniversary parties and graduation parties. Many of these events involve happy surprises, gift giving, and of course, lots of food.

We do these things to spend time together and honor one another, but none of these events is a replacement for a real relationship with one another.

The same is true for the celebrations and events and programs and restrictions that we might perform as a way of showing honor or obedience to God. These rituals or regulations or schedules or orders cannot take the place of a real, ongoing, growing relationship with the Lord Jesus Christ.

So celebrate however you like. Perform rituals if you must (if they are appropriate to what God has required of us). But always remember we are just living in the shadows—don't put too much stock in human-created programs and practices. Your real life is the one to come.

Lord, please help me to not be confused
about what You want from me. Amen. —M.L.

Come Near

Come near to God and he will come near to you.
JAMES 4:8

Sometimes we make our walk with God more complicated than it ever needs to be. But this advice in James does a wonderful job at summing up what followers of Jesus are to do, and what that will do for us.

"Come near to God." That's the part that's on us. How do we come near to God? We go where He is. We go to church to hear His Word taught, and we open our Bibles on our own to find Him in His Word again. We go where He's working, and we serve alongside Him, helping those who need it most. We go where He's comforting the sick and the suffering, and we put our arms around the ones He loves and has created, and we feel His arms around us all. We sing songs of praise to Him, and remember His beautiful, perfect qualities. We tell others what He has done for us. We pray, taking time to talk to Him and listen for His reply.

"And he will come near to you." He will be there for us. He will show up in our churches. He will be in the teaching. He will shape our words. He will guide our ministries. He will serve with us. He will talk to us.

Sounds pretty simple. And pretty wonderful.

Father God, come near. Amen. —M.L.

Missing Something?

"Are you tired? Worn out? Burned out on religion? Come to me. Get away with me and you'll recover your life. I'll show you how to take a real rest. Walk with me and work with me— watch how I do it. Learn the unforced rhythms of grace. I won't lay anything heavy or ill-fitting on you. Keep company with me and you'll learn to live freely and lightly."
MATTHEW 11:29–30 MSG

Got that chapter read in the Bible? Check. Good deed for the morning? Check. Hands folded in lap just so? Check. Head bowed? Check.

Got peace? Not so much.

Have we gotten so comfortable with a routine-like religion, we've left Jesus behind? Christ does want us to study His Word and pray, but it's easy to slip into a modern-day, weekly-planner mode where we just *do* for the Lord rather than living alongside the Lord. There's a big difference.

Can you hear the Lord talking to you in that still small voice? "Come to Me." "Get away with Me." "Walk with Me." "Work with Me." "Keep company with Me." We don't have to do it all on our own. In fact, He doesn't even want us to. He wants us to be with Him.

Ah yes, a relationship. So simple, we almost missed it.

Lord, I want to be with You.
Teach me Your ways. Amen. —A.H.

Beauty out of Chaos

The earth was a shapeless, chaotic mass,
with the Spirit of God brooding over the dark vapors.
GENESIS 1:2 TLB

A huge chunk of abandoned marble. Most people would see nothing beyond that intimidating sight of rough and formless stone. Except for Michelangelo—he saw a shepherd boy named David and a one-of-a-kind piece of art. His vision and skill and passion changed the world by inspiring everyone who has ever gazed upon the magnificence of *David*.

Humankind's heart aches to create beauty out of chaos. It is in our nature to do so, since God is the ultimate Creator and we are made in His image. That is why when we create something beautiful we feel satisfied and deeply connected to God.

When humankind fell from grace, this great rebellion could be seen as hopeless as a pile of formless rubble. And yet God saw hope, just as Michelangelo saw potential in that formless hunk of stone. God saw redemption and reconciliation, and He has invited us to allow Him to make beauty out of chaos, just as He did on that first day of Creation. What is your answer to Him?

Shall we allow Christ to make something truly magnificent out of our lives?

Yes, Lord, my life is Yours. Please create
something beautiful from it! Amen. —A.H.

Masquerade

I praise you because I am fearfully and wonderfully made;
your works are wonderful, I know that full well.

PSALM 139:14

People are notorious for pretending to be something they are not. Why? Because they sometimes worry they are deficient in some serious way. So they hide. They pretend. They boast. And sometimes they get angry at themselves and others.

Such agitation and striving and fretting is a waste of valuable time! God says we are fearfully and wonderfully made, and we need to take Him at His word. Ask God to show you who you were meant to be. What you are meant to do. He will show you, guide you, and love you through it all.

Psalm 139:16 reminds us that, "Your eyes saw my unformed body; all the days ordained for me were written in your book before one of them came to be."

So trust in the Lord that He will indeed follow through with His promises. If He made You, He will not leave you to wander the earth aimlessly. He will give you a beautiful purpose and everything you need to fulfill it!

I don't want to live a masquerade kind of life, Lord.
I want to know my purpose and trust You that
together we can fulfill it! Amen. —A.H.

A Divine Paradox!

Great is the Lord and most worthy of praise;
his greatness no one can fathom.

PSALM 145:3

The throne rooms of royalty are usually no less than resplendent with ornate ceilings, carved marble, and gilded glories of every kind. The apparel of monarchs is no less than opulent. Nothing would be too sumptuous for their tastes and desires.

And yet the King of kings and the Lord of lords came to live a very different life, full of humility, sorrow, and sacrifice. He wasn't born into wealth and privilege. In fact, His first crib was a trough in a stable. He never demanded opulent apparel or resplendent houses while He was here. He came to serve and to save us. But as a servant, Jesus also became our example, our Savior, and our true King. What a divine paradox!

It is easy to know the greatness of earthly kings and queens, since they are human and fallible, but God's greatness no one can fathom. He is full of mystery and glory and beauty beyond all our imaginings. Someday we will see our Lord again, and this time in all His glory. He is worthy not merely of our respect, but of our worship. Praise be to His holy name!

I am looking forward to heaven, Lord, and seeing You honored
and adored as the King of kings and Lord of lords! Amen. —A.H.

When All Goes Well

Consider it pure joy, my brothers and sisters, whenever you face trials of many kinds, because you know that the testing of your faith produces perseverance. Let perseverance finish its work so that you may be mature and complete, not lacking anything.

JAMES 1:2–4

The sun is out. You've just run a mile. Your stocks are up. You just got a promotion and your kids came home with straight As. Life is good. You feel as though you can do it all, have it all.

But beware. Sometimes when life gets too full of comfort it's tempting to think we can do life without God. And yet the truth is, even our very breath comes from God as well as every other blessing.

The Lord gives us good gifts, but we tend to grow closer to Him during lean times than lavish ones. Adversity can bring on strength of spirit, perseverance, and mature faith. The Lord does, of course, want us to enjoy our lives and delight in His many gifts, but He would like us to thank Him and commune with Him too. He wants to help and heal during hard times, redeem us during sinful times, and remind us of His presence during the generous times! He wants to be our friend, our God!

Lord, please keep me close to You no matter the season of my life. Amen. —A.H.

Not So Glamorous

*"Your kingdom come, your will be done,
on earth as it is in heaven."*
MATTHEW 6:10

"I want what I want, and I want it right now. Let's see. I want wealth. Lots of it. Good health so I can feel great while I'm spending it all. I want to be famous for being famous. Isn't that what everybody wants these days? Oh, and plenty of staff so I don't have to do any real work."

If we prayed like that, it would be like saying, "*My* kingdom come, *my* will be done." If you really could gather in everything you ever thought you desired, do you think it really would make your life story complete?

To live a self-gratifying, pleasure-seeking lifestyle may be the way of Hollywood, but if we look at the results of this kind of lifestyle, it doesn't appear nearly as glamorous as on the first blush. Not a lot of peace and joy coming out of Tinseltown. Or much enduring love for that matter.

Instead, wouldn't we want to trust in the One who knows us best and loves us better than anyone ever could? The Lord is the One who truly wants what is best for us, for now and all eternity. May we always say to the Lord, "Your will be done." It's the perfect beginning, middle, and end to our faith story!

*I give You carte blanche in my life, Lord.
Now and always! Amen. —A.H.*

Believe

Jesus asked, "Will you never believe in me unless you see miraculous signs and wonders?"
JOHN 4:48 NLT

People love a good superhero movie with mega special effects, right? We've always craved signs and wonders, not just ones that are pure illusion on the silver screen, but the real deal—the parting of the Red Sea, the mighty plagues of Egypt, pillars of fire, dramatic healings, the casting out of demons, and Elijah taken up in a whirlwind, to name a few. And God still reveals Himself in our modern world as well as in ancient times. But humankind seems to demand an endless supply of proof that God is there, that He cares for His creatures, and that He will return.

Christ wonders how many miracles He must perform before we have faith. In our prayers, do we constantly ask God for signs, or do we believe in Him and His saving grace? Maybe our prayer time would be better spent not in always begging for more proof and miracles, but begging for His mercy because of our lack of faith. Maybe some of our time could be spent in praising Him and thanking Him for all He has already done for us—blessings we can never repay, and grace we can never deserve!

Lord, may I always spend a portion of my quiet time in praise and thanksgiving. You alone are worthy of my worship! Amen. —A.H.

To Fret or Not to Fret

*Who of you by worrying can add
a single hour to your life?*
Luke 12:25

To fret or not to fret—that is the question. Our reply is usually no, but we do it anyway. Maybe we don't mean to. We have good intentions, but they slip away so easily—too easily. We get some bad news from the doctor, our spouse, or at work. Or we're on social media too long or we watch enough national news that before long our hands are wringing. Any number of things—including attacks by the enemy—can set us off into a fretting frenzy.

But Jesus' words in Luke summarize the situation very plainly and powerfully, "Who of you by worrying can add a single hour to your life?" Who indeed?

And every minute we are busy fretting takes away from time spent doing what is more important—like creating, laughing, playing, working, delighting, researching, loving, baking, singing, thanking, glorifying, exploring, eating, smiling, praising, sleeping, worshipping, celebrating, and well, living!

Maybe we should ask ourselves daily—do we really want to fritter our minutes, hours, and years away with fretting, when there is a world of wonder out there that God wants us to experience with Him?

*Help me to fret less, Lord,
and live by faith in You! Amen. —A.H.*

Apologetics versus Love

If I could speak all the languages of earth and of angels, but didn't love others, I would only be a noisy gong or a clanging cymbal.

1 CORINTHIANS 13:1 NLT

You're at the post office and as the line gets longer, the patience gets thinner. Yep, you can feel it—somebody is going to blow. When an argument does ensue, you cringe. Why? Because you know in your spirit, somebody is going to get hurt. Nobody likes a heated confrontation. Good rarely comes from it.

And so it goes with sharing our faith if done with too much bluster and pride and not enough humility and kindness. We can study apologetics until the cows come home, but if we have no love for the person we're witnessing to, it won't have much effect. Ask an adult why they came to Christ later in life, and many times she will tell you it had to do with someone loving her into the kingdom of God—not pushing, manipulating, guilting, arguing, or simply spouting all the correct answers.

Yes, the Holy Spirit can use our efforts, even when flawed. But a winsome attitude and love will help in winning people to Christ.

Lord, help me not to be a noisy gong but to love people as I tell them about the good news of Your Gospel! Amen. —A.H.

My Fashion Act

*But grow in the grace and knowledge of our Lord and Savior
Jesus Christ. To him be glory both now and forever! Amen.*
2 PETER 3:18

Life is full. Life is busy. But somehow you managed to get your fashion act together. Your new purse and shoes coordinate with your new dress. Check. Nine stores and five sales later, your accessories now harmonize with your ensemble. Check. You don the outfit and gaze into the mirror. Man, you look great!

Except there are still those little crinkles around your eyes, those tiny worry lines that never seem to go away. *Hmm.* We wonder—have we paid as much attention to getting our spiritual act together as our fashion act? Nothing wrong with buying a new dress, but paying attention to the details of our faith should be paramount. Why? Because anything that has any importance at all in this life is connected to the One who made us—to our ongoing relationship with the Lord. All other concerns fade in comparison.

Sure, buy that pretty, new dress in the window, but first ponder your relationship with Christ. Are you growing in the grace and knowledge of Him?

*Lord, help me to keep my priorities straight. When I gaze into the
mirror, may it always reflect You and Your love! Amen. —A.H.*

Stand Fast to Liberty!

Stand fast therefore in the liberty by which Christ has made us free, and do not be entangled again with a yoke of bondage.

GALATIANS 5:1 NKJV

We get too comfortable with spiritual bondages, don't we? We loathe them, but we sometimes tolerate them and make allowances for them just the same. Perhaps they have become such an intimate part of our lives that we can't let them go.

But that isn't the way of Christ. The Lord has truly set us free from bondages of all kinds. Humankind is very clever and sly at creating new kinds of oppression or guilting us back into old ones. But we need to stand fast in our liberty. Yes, the chains are broken. The gate has been thrown wide open. Let us never walk back inside and slam the door because prison life is all we know, or we are tricked into thinking there is a strange kind of comfort in its confining space and miseries. May we live so free in Christ that others will want to accept Him and storm their own prison doors!

Lord Jesus, thank You for setting me free for all time! Watch over me so that I do not return to my old ways and burdens. Remind me daily that I am truly set free in You! Amen. —A.H.

Juicy Ripe Peaches—Ahh!

Brethren, do not be children in understanding; however,
in malice be babes, but in understanding be mature.
1 CORINTHIANS 14:20 NKJV

Have you ever reached up and plucked an unripe (and greenish) peach off a tree? Yeah, those little buggers are as hard as stones. If you threw one like a baseball, people would be wise to run for their lives!

However, if you walk away from that peach for a while, and let it do what God intended for it to do—that is, get kissed by the sun and fully ripened on the branch—you will be able to harvest a piece of fruit that is mature and memorable, not to mention sweet, juicy, and, you guessed it, usable. You can now make peach preserves, peach pie, peach cobbler, peach tea, old-fashioned peach ice cream, peach everything. People will respond, "Yes, please!"

That's the way of growing a mature faith in Christ. We become Son-kissed and memorable and usable. People will run toward you, not away from you. They will look at your life and say, "Yes, please!"

I want to be mature in my faith and usable for Your kingdom
and glory, Lord. Help me to accomplish this with Your help!
In Jesus' name I pray. Amen. —A.H.

Not the "H" Word!

Do not forget to show hospitality to strangers, for by so doing some people have shown hospitality to angels without knowing it.
HEBREWS 13:2

Hospitality. Oh dear. Not that word. Guests can be gloriously fun, but after a few days they have the potential to become as pleasant as rotten mackerel! For instance, your overnight guest unexpectedly throws up all over your expensive new comforter. The neighbor's kid—who's kind of grumpy—keeps coming over for breakfast before school (uninvited) because his mom doesn't seem to have the money to feed him. The neighbor lady you invited over for coffee and cake has so many health issues (and phobias) you're not sure what to do or say. You just suddenly feel tired.

Bottom line—hospitality ain't easy. Because people are messy. And yet in various scriptures, God encourages us to welcome folks into our homes and hearts. The Lord even tells us that sometimes those guests might be visiting angels. Now that adds a new level of pressure, eh?

You need to have faith in the Lord to extend hospitality, since any number of things can go wrong. Ask the Lord for discernment when choosing who to invite. Then ask for good health, creative ideas, stamina, and a genuine love for helping people!

Lord, sometimes I don't feel I have the gift of hospitality.
But if You will help me, I will do my best because
I love You dearly. Amen. —A.H.

That Mighty Truth

Cast all your anxiety on him because he cares for you.
1 PETER 5:7

Anxiety is that nasty, sweaty feeling that makes you think something is about to go very wrong. Or maybe that foul feeling has already turned into an avalanche of tribulation. Yikes!

But take heart, the Lord says to cast all of your burdens on Him.

Why would Jesus choose to take on such misery? Because the Lord cares for us—profoundly. Have we infused our innermost being with that mighty truth? Okay. Maybe. Yes. Even when we wake up in the middle of the night drenched in fear? Then why do we take our anxiety back later? Is it because we don't think the Lord works fast enough or He won't handle our problems in the right way? Is it because we think He has more pressing concerns? Is it because we question His true character?

If the Lord asks us to cast all our anxiety on Him, He means it. He's powerful enough and holy enough and wise enough to take all our convoluted and chronic and confusing problems and make something beautiful out of it all.

He wants us to trust Him now, trust Him always. . .

Lord, I admit that sometimes I am riddled with doubts and worry and questions. I don't always trust You like I should. I do believe. Help my unbelief! Amen. —A.H.

The Wonderful Things!

For ever since the creation of the world His invisible attributes,
His eternal power and divine nature, have been clearly seen,
being understood through His workmanship [all His creation, the
wonderful things that He has made], so that they [who fail to
believe and trust in Him] are without excuse and without defense.
ROMANS 1:20 AMP

Sometimes we have faith in the tiniest things. The most fragile things. And sometimes we even conjure up faith in the most ill-advised and futile things!

But God is truly worthy of our faith. Because of God's magnificent workmanship we can see that He is powerful, eternal, and divine. All those who refuse to believe and trust in the Lord will be without excuse. They have seen His glorious creation, they've taken pleasure in it all, but they have refused to acknowledge the Creator of such magnificent gifts. May we always praise Him for His majesty, love Him with our whole hearts, and accept His saving grace through Christ!

Father God, may I always rise up in the morning with a thankful
heart when I see Your creation. I am in awe of all that You
have made and given to us to delight in. Help me to share my
testimony with others, that they may open their eyes to You
and Your wonderment and then open their hearts to Your
mercy and grace. In Jesus' name I pray. Amen. —A.H.

Those He Loves

My child, don't reject the LORD's discipline, and don't be upset when he corrects you. For the LORD corrects those he loves, just as a father corrects a child in whom he delights.
PROVERBS 3:11–12 NLT

Your little Jimmy yanks his hand from yours and runs into speeding traffic. The cars slam on their brakes just in time to avoid a horrific accident. But you know—since you love Jimmy more than he can even realize—that there's going to be some sort of discipline for his defiant and dangerous behavior. And so there should be. Good parents wouldn't shrug their shoulders and let Jimmy think all was fine with his conduct. If so, Jimmy would probably do it again and perhaps try something even more perilous.

Spiritually, aren't we a little like Jimmy-boy? Sometimes we run headlong into what we know is sinful and deadly, but defiantly, we choose to do it anyway. In times like these, may we never reject the Lord's correction. He disciplines us because of His great love for us. And wouldn't it be better to be disciplined by a holy God who loves us and delights in us than to be praised by the deceiver—Satan?

Lord, may I always welcome Your loving and perfectly-timed corrections. Amen. —A.H.

The Lord's Promise

We all, like sheep, have gone astray, each of us has turned to our own way; and the LORD has laid on him the iniquity of us all.
ISAIAH 53:6

People like to go their own way, do their own thing. But it's obvious from watching the news that this broken world is in desperate need of a Savior. Who will the world choose? Nature can be full of breathtaking marvels, but it can't save us. Doing good works, no matter how selfless they may seem, can't save us. Man-made faiths can't save us. Only Christ has the supernatural power to save.

People might ask, "But how can I know for sure that the way of Christ is the one true way? Is He worthy of my faith?" Our Lord says, "Ask and it will be given to you; seek and you will find; knock and the door will be opened to you. For everyone who asks receives; the one who seeks finds; and to the one who knocks, the door will be opened" (Matthew 7:7–8 NIV). If you seek the Lord, you will find Him. It is the Lord's promise to everyone—and to you.

I know and love You, Lord. Please show me how to be a witness to others that they might know the way, the truth, and the life. Amen. —A.H.

A Day in the Life

Pile your troubles on GOD's shoulders—
he'll carry your load, he'll help you out.
PSALM 55:22 MSG

Your hand is balled up. Each finger is curling inward so hard that your fist is turning white. You can't seem to help it. Stomach tight. Eyes wide. Sweaty nights. A few nightmares to add to the miserable, hot mess. You're ready to fight, ready to flee. But truth be known, you'd rather just curl up into a fetal position under the table. So what is this thing—this malady?

It's called another day of life.

But that is so far from the way God wants us to live. When He says in His Word to pile our troubles on Him, He really means it. Why? Because He cares for us just as any loving parent does. Only infinitely more. The Lord doesn't want us to stress over life until it's impossible to live.

There is a big, bold, and beautiful life out there for you, so ask God to show you the way to be free of cares. That way you can concentrate on what is excellent—His good and perfect will.

I am ready to be free of worry, Lord. Help me to untighten my fist,
climb out from under that table of fear, and live my life for You.
I'm excited to see what we will do next! Amen. —A.H.

Beloved Friend

"Whoever has my commands and keeps them is the one who loves me. The one who loves me will be loved by my Father, and I too will love them and show myself to them."

JOHN 14:21

You've known your best bud, Bev, since grade school. People said you were two peas in a pod, but now, years later, you've grown to love each other like sisters. The more you get to know each other, the more you open up and trust each other. You've become so devoted that you wouldn't do anything to hurt the other. You love so deeply that Bev's joy is now *your* joy. You might even think, "What can I do today to bring Bev some special happiness?"

As you grow in your relationship with Christ, there are a few similarities with our earthly friendships. Are you so devoted to Christ that you wouldn't do anything to hurt the relationship? The closer you get to the Lord, do you trust Him more completely? Do you love Christ so deeply that His joy is *Your* joy? Do you ask, "What can I do today to bring Him some special happiness?"

Yes, Jesus is God and is worthy of our most earnest reverence, but Jesus also calls us friends.

Lord, may I always approach You with awe, but hold You in my heart as the dearest friend I'll ever have. Amen. —A.H.

Beautiful and Usable

He cuts off every branch in me that bears no fruit,
while every branch that does bear fruit he prunes
so that it will be even more fruitful.

JOHN 15:2

Ever bought one of those rock tumblers for your child? The hobbyist tosses in handfuls of common pebbles and out comes a little pile of smooth, gemstone-like rocks! There are a few downsides, though. This tumbling business is sometimes a noisy affair, and it can take a long time for the stones to be smoothed and made beautiful and usable.

What a good analogy for how it is to grow in our faith in Christ. Yes, to become beautiful and usable we will need some spiritual smoothing, and it might take a while. Not to mention the fact that banging around in a tumbler—to wear off our errant ways—is usually not a pain-free ride!

But the process is necessary. As John puts it, the Lord prunes us to produce fruit—not just any fruit, but big, luscious, sun-kissed fruit the whole world yearns for. In this way, the Lord is made irresistible to humanity—and Christ is just what this broken and hurting world really needs.

Lord, thank You for Your loving and careful pruning
so that I can produce a beautiful harvest of
good fruit for Your glory. Amen. —A.H.

A New Kind of Tired

Instead, they were longing for a better country—
a heavenly one. Therefore God is not ashamed to be
called their God, for he has prepared a city for them.
HEBREWS 11:16

Yes, you're trying to look vibrant and vital, trying to fit everything in, trying, trying, trying, but you look into the mirror and you have that beaten-down, thrown-under-the-bus look. You never seem to say the right things. People cut you off in traffic. Dismiss your kind deed. Rebuff your attempt at sharing the Gospel. People forget to call, forget to say they love you. You feel bewildered, unappreciated, and maybe even invisible. Basically, you're exhausted from not feeling in sync with the ebb and flow of this fallen life.

It really is okay not to fit in perfectly here. We really aren't meant to get too comfortable on this side of eternity. We are earth travelers, waiting with expectation for the home Christ has promised—a new heaven and a new earth!

In the meantime, cry out to the Lord for mercy—as people have done throughout the centuries. He hears your plea. He sees your pain. He understands your tears. He will hold you tightly.

Trust. Know.

Lord, I am world weary. Please tuck me into
the curve of Your mighty arm! Amen. —A.H.

When We Do Right

For the LORD God is our sun and our shield.
He gives us grace and glory. The LORD will withhold
no good thing from those who do what is right.
PSALM 84:11 NLT

Have you ever insulted someone right to her face—maybe even in front of a crowd—and the moment the nasty words came out of your mouth, your stomach lurched with regret?

We know it—soul deep—when we've done wrong. If we have accepted Christ, we have been given the Holy Spirit, and with His help we can know good from bad, right from wrong. Even though we won't be perfect while residing on this fallen earth, we can sincerely pray for direction and choose what is right. And we can become righteous through our faith. Even though Abraham was not without transgressions God referred to him as righteous because of his faith.

We can choose to worship the Lord, to read His living Word, and to spend time with Him. We can decide to follow Christ and His teachings and to live lives of integrity, kindness, and faith. May we then enjoy the blessings that come from obeying Him!

Forgive me for my trespasses, Lord. I truly want
to do all that is right, and I want You to grow me
into a strong woman of faith! Amen. —A.H.

Treading Lightly

To slander no one, to be peaceable and considerate,
and always to be gentle toward everyone.

TITUS 3:2

People's spirits are sometimes like strewn petals—so we should tread lightly—for they bruise easily. We don't know all of what a person has been through. We don't know the cruelties she has endured. We can't know unless we have lived her life. So it is always better to err on the side of gentleness when dealing with our fellow man or woman.

Have you ever offered a cup of kindness or tender words to someone, and then later discovered that the woman had greatly appreciated what you'd done because she had just recovered from a serious illness or perhaps was trying to deal with the death of a loved one? Yes, she had been in great need of that gentle touch, and your spirit was willing to come to her aid. You must have sighed deep within, knowing you had made God smile. Then you might wonder, how many times have you offered kindness and gentle words, without ever knowing the final story? The ripple effects of being gentle and peaceable and kind are far reaching—more than we can ever imagine.

Holy Spirit, help me not to trample on people's
tender spirits, but show me how to be gentle
and humble in all my ways. Amen. —A.H.

The World's Weights and Measures

*Am I now trying to win the approval of human beings, or of God?
Or am I trying to please people? If I were still trying to please
people, I would not be a servant of Christ.*

GALATIANS 1:10

If you compiled a list of all your top goals and dreams, what would it look like? What's at the pinnacle of your heart's hidden desires? Would you be willing to share that list on social media? Do you think the list would please God or man?

Listening to the whispers of the world and the enemy's lies, we get the impression that doing God's will translates into living a small, trivial kind of life. But by whose weights and measures do we decide what is small and what is important? A world that cares nothing for God can cook up various pleasures and comfort-filled living, but not real contentment. Watch the news and read about the lives of celebrities and you will come away with the truth that only God's way is the right way. Only His plans have everything we need for heartfelt laughter, for peace like a river, and for real love that lasts an eternity. The world's sparkly trinkets will always dim in comparison to the genuine treasures of God's kingdom!

*Lord, I want to live my life by Your weights
and measures, not mine. Amen. —A.H.*

The Beauty of Reconciliation

*Be kind and compassionate to one another,
forgiving each other, just as in Christ God forgave you.*
EPHESIANS 4:32

Forgiveness and reconciliation are complicated, uncomfortable, and messy. Passing over these lessons and skipping to other biblical teachings might be easier to deal with. Like maybe eating less food to avoid the sin of gluttony? But that one is hard too.

It's important not to avoid the difficult lesson of forgiveness and reconciliation. Say you and your friend have offended each other and you've had a falling-out. You no longer speak to each other, and reconciliation seems impossible.

Do remember that God is the supreme authority on forgiveness, and He's a real expert when it comes to the impossible. He can help. In fact, He would love to help you both. Ask Him. Trust Him for a good outcome. And then with that sincere prayer in your heart and a warm smile on your face, offer to buy your friend a lovely lunch at her favorite place. See what mighty miracle the Lord can do. Sometimes it just takes that first step of faith.

*Lord, I'm a little scared, but I'm willing to take the first step.
I'm going to trust You to help bring my broken relationship
to a beautiful place of understanding, forgiveness,
and reconciliation. Amen. —A.H.*

It Is Priceless!

*Therefore encourage one another and build
each other up, just as in fact you are doing.*
1 THESSALONIANS 5:11

A friend that you care about deeply has recently experienced a series of very unhappy events in her life. You have it in your power to put some of the light back in her eyes with some encouraging words, a cup of coffee—the seriously good kind—and maybe even a little surprise gift. Are you willing to do it?

Surely the answer is yes. That is one lovely way to fulfill 1 Thessalonians 5:11. But what if you are so downhearted, so physically tired, and so spiritually drained that you are barely able to meet the needs of others? Not even your best friend's needs?

Well then, it's time to spend some quiet, one-on-one time with the Savior. Talk to Him. Lean on Him. Trust Him. Rest in Him. Then when you've found your strength and groove and smile again, you can once again know the wonderful feeling that comes from encouraging and lifting others up. The smile you put on her face will carry no price tag, because it will be priceless!

*Jesus, may I always rest in Your mighty arms so thoroughly,
trust in You so profoundly, that when people need my
encouragement, I am ready, willing, and able! Amen. —A.H.*

A Life of Beauty

And we know that all things work together for good to those who love God, to those who are the called according to His purpose.
ROMANS 8:28 NKJV

All days don't seem to be created equal. We may rise up with hope, but sometimes life gets complicated and weary and confusing. Trust God. Give Him your day. Even *those* days. . .

Those hurting, "I can't seem to do anything right" days. Those lazy, "I can't seem to get out of bed" days. Those crabby, "Stay out of my way so nobody will get hurt" days. Those confusing, "I don't know who I am anymore" days. Those disappointing, "I fell into a sin that I vowed never to revisit" days. Those "I am a strong Christian, but today doubt crept into my spirit" days. And those "I'm afraid of everything. Is there such a thing as life-phobia?" days.

Do you love God enough to trust Him with all your days and nights—no matter what kind? If You love Him, He will work all things for good in your life. It's a promise He will keep. With supernatural power He can transform what seems ordinary and human and fallen into something holy and peaceful and usable—a real life of beauty.

Lord, I can't do life alone. Please rescue me from myself and create in me a life of beauty! Amen. —A.H.

How Not to Be Foolish

Don't be quick to fly off the handle. Anger boomerangs.
You can spot a fool by the lumps on his head.
ECCLESIASTES 7:9 MSG

Foolhardiness comes naturally to us. But then some people seem predisposed to folly, like having gout on a big toe! Even people who think they are founts of wisdom can be found sneaking around, sipping from a well of foolishness from time to time. *Hmm.* How can anyone hope to be wise then? There are many ways, and one is not to fly off the handle over every little thing!

So what do you do when anger flares up and you suddenly feel like screaming, hitting something, or spewing ill-advised language? The world would say to take anger management classes. But our hearts would say that we should seek a closer walk with the Lord by pouring out more prayer and less anger. Christ may ask a few questions, though, like what is behind this curtain of anger? Are you harboring bitterness from the past?

Let the Lord light up the dark, pain-filled crevices of your heart with His divine love and forgiveness and healing. Then trust Him as you prepare yourself to be cherished and challenged and changed!

I know I have anger issues, Lord. Please help me.
I can no longer do this alone. Amen. —A.H.

The Ultimate Love Gift

*He personally carried our sins in his body on the cross
so that we can be dead to sin and live for what
is right. By his wounds you are healed.*
1 PETER 2:24 NLT

Have you ever done a really great deed, and your best efforts got squashed? Perhaps your kindness got misunderstood, scoffed at, or worse, completely rejected? That would be devastating, wouldn't it—to have your love-gift trampled? Perhaps you would have a hard time recovering. Maybe you wouldn't want to offer any more kind deeds. It's just too hurtful emotionally—too risky.

Jesus knows how that feels. He offered us the most generous, compassionate, and sacrificial gift that humankind has ever known or will ever know. Christ suffered agonizing torture and humiliation and death so that we might truly live in a way that has been lost since the garden of Eden. And yet so many people reject His finest gift! They stubbornly and arrogantly and faithlessly choose to go it alone—just as Adam and Eve did.

Are you grateful that Jesus conquered death through His resurrection? And that when we by faith accept His gift of salvation, we get to enjoy the wonders of eternal life in heaven? What have you personally done with God's love-gift?

*Jesus, I accept Your love-gift of salvation. I love You!
May I always live for You! Amen. —A.H.*

Celebrate!

"But the father said to his servants, 'Quick! Bring the best robe and put it on him. Put a ring on his finger and sandals on his feet. Bring the fattened calf and kill it. Let's have a feast and celebrate. For this son of mine was dead and is alive again; he was lost and is found.' So they began to celebrate."
LUKE 15:22–24

Most people love a great party, and the Bible mentions all kinds of celebrations. In the story of the prodigal son, the father was so jubilant over his son's homecoming—a moment that he thought was lost forever—that he naturally wanted to rejoice with a big gathering of his friends.

Yes, we should rejoice over God's blessings and not fret that we will lose them, because not only will that attitude put a wet blanket on a fine celebration, it will mean we don't fully trust in God's ongoing provision.

May we make merry over the harvest, a healing, the return of the prodigal, the miracle—whatever it is that we are so deeply grateful to God for. But whatever we do, let us not forget to invite the Lord to our celebrations!

Thank You, Lord God, for all the wonderful blessings in my life. I want to celebrate Your goodness and mercy and provision! Amen. —A.H.

Please, Fill My Cup, Lord!

You serve me a six-course dinner right in front of my enemies.
You revive my drooping head; my cup brims with blessing.
PSALM 23:5 MSG

Do you ever feel that your spirit is empty? That you have nothing left to give? You've got no more encouragement to provide, no more money to contribute, no more listening ear, no more consoling and hopeful words to say, and maybe not even any more prayers to offer up? That big, sweet-smelling teapot of kindness—that you kept pouring and pouring—is not only empty, but you discovered that somebody has stolen your pot!

It's time to tell the Lord all about it. Sit before Him, knowing of His great love for You, relishing the way He's come to Your rescue, time and time again through the years, and trusting in your heart that He will protect you, comfort you, and even offer you a feast in front of your enemies. The Lord will lift your drooping head and restore you. And the Lord will find that pot—which the enemy stole—and fill it up to overflowing!

I praise You, Lord, for I know in Your mercy You will miraculously turn my burden into a blessing! Amen. —A.H.

Time

I cried out to him with my mouth; his praise was on my tongue. If I had cherished sin in my heart, the Lord would not have listened; but God has surely listened and has heard my prayer.

PSALM 66:17–19

Our society has gotten maniacal about time—so the solution is to multitask. But why do we insist that life isn't productive or satisfying unless we're doing a dozen things at once? Why can't we slow down or cherish the moment? Why are we so hopped-up on busyness that we can't listen to our family, friends, or God anymore? When we crash in bed at night, we're exhausted, but we can't sleep because we're still flying around in our spirits, our little propellers spinning nervously. Maybe we think that sleep is a total waste of our time!

God sees time from a different vantage point—through the lens of eternity—and unlike us, He does know how to listen. In fact, it's one of His specialties. But first, He asks us, "Have we cherished sin in our hearts?" *Hmm.* Guess we'd need some repentance first, then we could move forward, talking to the Lord, hearing and learning, resting and trusting.

There will never be a better use of our time than to walk in the divine ways of our Lord!

Jesus, please help me to remember these important precepts and act on them! Amen. —A.H.

The People of Joy!

Let the heavens be glad, and the earth rejoice! Let the sea and everything in it shout his praise! Let the fields and their crops burst out with joy! Let the trees of the forest sing for joy before the LORD, for he is coming! He is coming to judge the earth. He will judge the world with justice, and the nations with his truth.

PSALM 96:11–13 NLT

We have every reason to be the harvesters of great joy! And after a bountiful season of happiness, most generous people want to share their abundance with others. You might think, "That sounds a little over the top." Are you feeling a little left behind on the joy train? But why? When we love our Lord fully, we will not fear. If we trust Jesus with all our hearts, then we have every reason to be acquainted with much delight in our souls, since through Christ, we will know life for all time. That is, life lived in truth, justice, and pure love. So, cherish the promise. Look forward to the journey. And share this good news with abandon!

Lord of my life, may the joy I have in You show in everything I do. Please help me to share that joy with everyone around me. Amen. —M.L.

The God We Worship

God's voice thunders in marvelous ways;
he does great things beyond our understanding.
JOB 37:5

God is so magnificent, and His creation continues to astound, mystify, and inspire us! So much to behold, it can take our breath away. So much to enjoy, we cannot fathom it all. So much to be thankful to Him for, we can barely find the words for all these earthly treasures. . .

Sunbeams dancing on the forest floor, and the feathered finery of a peacock's plumage.

The aroma of bergamot wafting from a teapot, and the clean tang of earth-air just before a rain.

The woolly cuteness of chipmunks and miniature owls and wombats.

Vistas opening to jagged mountain cliffs, and copper canyons dressed in snowy ermine coats.

Glistening dewdrops on petals, and moonlight shimmers across the sea.

The whisper glide of a swan across a misty pool, and rainbows crossing a plunging waterfall.

The artistic wonder of sunsets and gems, and the engineering marvels of nests and dragonflies.

Lord, You have more wow factor than the world could ever dream of! Your divine handiwork and power is beyond our understanding. Praise be to Your mighty name!

You, God, are glorious in all You do. You are the God we love,
the God we trust! So worthy are You of our praise! Amen. —A.H.

We Sing of Life

But Jesus answered them, saying, "The hour has come that the
Son of Man should be glorified. Most assuredly, I say to you,
unless a grain of wheat falls into the ground and dies,
it remains alone; but if it dies, it produces much grain."
JOHN 12:23–24 NKJV

There in that garden tomb in Israel, the air is as still as death itself, and yet the stone hollow sings of life. The morning light flows in, and yet you sense that it is the very illumination of heaven pouring into that open vault. Yes, that empty tomb whispers a holy-hushed wonder, yet it shouts songs of victory—the resurrection of Jesus Christ! He died that we may have life—abundant life! What glory, what wonder. Praise be to His name!

So when this fractured world seems to be violently shaking itself apart, and the evil seems to be lurking—ready to lunge at you at every turn—remember that light of heaven. Remember that song of life. Remember the empty tomb of Christ. We can walk away from that place unchained and changed forever if we embrace His gift, His love, His life. Believe.

O Lord, I am so grateful that You didn't stay in that grave, but that
You rose again. I accept Your unfathomable gift of salvation.
I too now sing of life in You. Hallelujah! Amen. —A.H.

An Eternity of Joy!

He was despised and rejected by humankind, a man of suffering, and familiar with pain. Like one from whom people hide their faces he was despised, and we held him in low esteem.

ISAIAH 53:3–5

Sometimes life feels like a ship's anchor—not an anchor holding you steady but one that is hanging around your neck and pulling you under! So when that happens, you might need to sit down and have a good cry.

Life can be pain-filled, confusing, and more than a little scary. Knowing that Jesus understands our suffering brings us comfort. While living on earth among us, the Lord didn't get a reputation for being a man who spent a lot of time laughing or joking or acting particularity merry. Jesus knew what He was destined to do—and what He was willing to do—and yet the horrific events that transpired did indeed bring Him great sorrow.

So when you ache all over with a serious case of life-sickness, know that Jesus understands every kind of pain—in body and mind and spirit. Not just a nebulous idea of what human agony might be like from afar, but Jesus loved us enough to *live* all the pain—for us. Because of His willingness to be a man of sorrows, He has brought us an eternity of joy!

How grateful I am for You, Lord. May I be comforted by the knowledge of Your sacrificial love. Amen. —A.H.

A Wily Thing

Pride goes before destruction,
a haughty spirit before a fall.
PROVERBS 16:18

Pride is such a crafty beast—it chases and teases almost as if it's harmless—but if you're not diligent in keeping it at bay, the creature will devour you.

Too dramatic, you say? If we claim to be honest folk, then we have to admit that from time to time, haughty eyes have looked back at us in the mirror. The insidious nature of smugness and pomposity creeps in like radon vapors across a cellar floor. If it's there, it can be deadly. But the difference is you can't see gas, but you can see pride! And it can get pretty ugly.

So how does one steer clear of the devious ways of the world? Stay close to Christ, through prayer and fellowship and reading His Word. Maybe even stay accountable to a few godly friends who can tell you honestly if you've been romancing pride.

If you are guilty, repent. And then ask the Lord to help you be more watchful in the future. Even when you think you've gone too far, or you've sinned too much, trust God to bring you back home.

Lord, help me to recognize pride if it rises up in me, and please give me the strength and will to send it packing! Amen. —A.H.

Transitions

For the word of the LORD is right and true;
he is faithful in all he does.
PSALM 33:4

So you've trusted God with the little stuff. You've even had faith when something big came along to tempt you or taunt you or torment you. Now you see a milestone ahead, but it doesn't feel like a fun adventure—more like standing on the edge of an abyss with no bridge in sight.

Yep, it's retirement time.

People say you're supposed to live it up now. Reinvent yourself. Get a new look. Volunteer. Travel. Play with the grandkids. But no matter how much you feel like you should be celebrating, you find yourself staring at the wall. Nothing motivates you. No pressing need to roll out of bed. You feel used up. Tossed out. Like the best of you is all behind you. What in the world do you do now?

Trust God.

We can trust Him as we move through the many seasons of change. Marriage. Kids. Empty nest. Retirement. Assisted living. Hospice. Heaven. Unlike what the world has to offer, God is faithful. Period. He will bring you through as He has promised to do time and time again. Now is the time to trust. He is right here. . .

Lord, I'm in the middle of this new season in my life, and I'm
scared. Please be ever near me. I love You! Amen. —A.H.

Knowing the One You Trust

Very early in the morning, while it was still dark, Jesus got up, left the house and went off to a solitary place, where he prayed.

MARK 1:35

If some random person came up to you and said he wanted you to trust him with your money or your house or even say, your very life, what would you do? You'd probably say, "Are you nuts?" Or you'd speed-walk the other way. Why? Because he's a stranger. You don't know him well enough to trust him with anything, let alone something precious!

If we say that we trust God with our daily lives, wouldn't we want to make sure He wasn't a stranger to us? Wouldn't we want to get to know Him and all the many divine facets of His character? To get to know the "who" of God would naturally be a faith builder, right?

One way we can get to know God better is to follow Jesus' example while He walked this earth. We can go to a solitary place, read His Word, and pray. Life will never feel more beautiful or more peace-filled than when we fellowship with the Lord.

I never want us to feel like strangers, Lord. My heart's desire is to have a more loving fellowship with You, and in that "getting to know You" closeness, may I come to trust You more! Amen. —A.H.

An Impression of Innocence

For such people are false apostles, deceitful workers,
masquerading as apostles of Christ. And no wonder,
for Satan himself masquerades as an angel of light.
2 CORINTHIANS 11:13–14

A blanket bog—such as the ones found in Scotland and in other countries—can give the appearance of being a pleasant place for a hike or a stroll. But bogs can be deadly places, especially for the uninformed and ill-prepared. Bogs can pull you under and swallow you up whole if you misstep.

There are innumerable, innocent-appearing, earthly hazards. They are everywhere, just like spiritual dangers. Terrifying, you might say. Yes, indeed! But nothing we can't handle with the Lord's help. We need to be informed and prepared, as Paul mentions in 2 Corinthians. Some of the things we lustfully desire aren't good for us, as the Bible says. And some of the things we worship and the people we listen to—including false prophets—will lead us to destruction. Not fun to hear about, but it's always better to know the truth than to topple into a deadly spiritual bog!

Oh, Lord, please keep me safe from the deceiver and all the things that can bring peril to my soul. May I walk with You all the days of my life. In Jesus' holy name I pray. Amen. —A.H.

Joy to the Lord!

But those who wish to boast should boast in this alone: that they truly know me and understand that I am the LORD who demonstrates unfailing love and who brings justice and righteousness to the earth, and that I delight in these things. I, the LORD, have spoken!

JEREMIAH 9:24 NLT

If we're brutally honest, sometimes our prayers to God disintegrate into "gimme all the goodies" sessions. We might neglect the praise and repentance and thanksgiving and listening, while hoping that the Lord will do our bidding. That is, to bring us all the little—and big—desires of our heart.

The Lord does welcome our requests, but do we ever wake up in the morning and wonder, "What can I do to bring joy to the Lord today? Not in a vain attempt to make myself look holy in front of all the right people. Not in a frantic effort to earn my way into heaven, which is impossible, but just to thank You, Jesus, for all You've done for me!"

Now *that's* a pondering that would surely give God something to smile about!

Lord Jesus, I am happy to boast that I know You, and I'm excited to share the good news of Your justice and righteousness and unfailing love! Amen. —A.H.

A Little Christmas Every Day

The Word became flesh and made his dwelling among us.
We have seen his glory, the glory of the one and only Son,
who came from the Father, full of grace and truth.

JOHN 1:14

Don't you just love Christmas? From the fragrant boughs of evergreen draped across the mantel to the candles flickering softly in the windows. From the heartwarming carols about "goodwill toward men" to the smells of turkey roasting in the oven. From the star in the east to the manger where the King of kings slept. All of it. Beautiful. Just beautiful.

If we know Christ, we have all things bright and beautiful to show the world, and we have good news that cannot be contained! We have seen His glory! Let's show this old, aching world how to celebrate this profoundly meaningful holiday. And we can show them not just one day a year, but a little bit every single day—in the way we smile, the way we love, and in the way we tell them the truth about Christ!

Yes, tell the world—Christmas isn't just a holiday. To follow Christ is a love affair of the heart that lasts for all time! Merry Christmas!

Thank You, Jesus, for creating a holiday with
such eternal significance, such love! Amen. —A.H.

Choices

There's more to come: We continue to shout our praise even when we're hemmed in with troubles, because we know how troubles can develop passionate patience in us, and how that patience in turn forges the tempered steel of virtue, keeping us alert for whatever God will do next. In alert expectancy such as this, we're never left feeling shortchanged. Quite the contrary— we can't round up enough containers to hold everything God generously pours into our lives through the Holy Spirit!

ROMANS 5:4–5 MSG

So many choices in life. Chocolate truffle ice cream, or familiar vanilla? The friendly shoes, or the spiky, chic ones? The tearoom for lunch, or the '50s diner?

But some life-choices aren't so frivolous—they are spiritual in nature and have more serious consequences. Will I choose to let God use my various trials and disappointments to mold me into something beautiful, or will I fall into bitterness?

We may think our retorts and reactions are out of our control, but they aren't. We have a choice. How will I react to this hardship? Will I let it define me as a woman of anger and resentment, or will I let it create a passionate patience in my soul? Will I choose the way of folly, or the way of faith?

Lord, in the midst of trials, I choose to wait on You with excited anticipation! Amen. —A.H.

Stand Strong!

And that about wraps it up. God is strong, and He wants you strong. So take everything the Master has set out for you, well-made weapons of the best materials. And put them to use so you will be able to stand up to everything the Devil throws your way. This is no afternoon athletic contest that we'll walk away from and forget about in a couple of hours. This is for keeps, a life-or-death fight to the finish against the Devil and all his angels.
EPHESIANS 6:10–12 MSG

If you get a kick out of online research, try searching the "most dangerous roads on earth." You might not sleep for weeks. Some highways are so remote that cellphones would be a joke, and running out of gas is unthinkable. Some roads are narrow with cliffs, hairpin turns, and no guardrails. And yet another road might take you through a war zone or sweep your car out to sea.

Sounds as fearsome as watching the evening news!

Yes, this life-road of ours is spiritually treacherous. But instead of being paralyzed with panic, we need to stay strong, by faithfully clinging to Christ as our guide, by using His living Word as a road map, and by praying for the salvation of the world!

Lord, I choose to cling to You in these dark and scary times. Together we can stand strong against the enemy! Amen. —A.H.

The Fine Fellowship

And let us consider [thoughtfully] how we may encourage one another to love and to do good deeds, not forsaking our meeting together [as believers for worship and instruction], as is the habit of some, but encouraging one another; and all the more [faithfully] as you see the day [of Christ's return] approaching.

HEBREWS 10:24–25 AMP

Yes, it's tempting to linger over that second and third cup of coffee on Sunday morning instead of going to church, but God encourages us to live differently, as Hebrews 10 says. Have the coffee, but don't forget the fellowshipping!

Still, many people ask the question, "Why do I need church anyway?"

There are plenty of good reasons. Here are a few:

> To hear the Word of God read aloud.
> To help escape the traps of false doctrines and false prophets, cults, and deceitful spirits.
> To praise, thank, and worship God—the Maker of all!
> To fellowship with other people who are like-minded.
> To stay accountable to fellow believers.
> To learn the precepts of Christ and encourage one another in our faith.

How can we refuse this valuable and beautiful gift? So, yes, let's pour the good coffee and enjoy the fine fellowship! Do I hear an amen?

Lord, help me not to forsake Your house of worship but to be more faithful in attending! Amen. —A.H.

Take His Hand

Have I not commanded you? Be strong and courageous.
Do not be afraid; do not be discouraged, for the LORD
your God will be with you wherever you go.
JOSHUA 1:9

Have you had one of *those* days? You know, when you're convinced the whole world is against you? Oh, and you're tired and irritable and you've got this nagging feeling you've mislaid something. . . What is it? Oh yeah—it's you! Then, if that's not enough, you lift your head off the kitchen table, stare at the overflowing trash can and say, "Why is that garbage bin always full, while my cup of patience and energy and faith is nearly empty?"

Oh, Lord, I need help!

Even as faithful Christians, we've all had days of exhaustion, confusion, doubts, and impatience. We've all felt alone and a little scared. Okay, a lot scared. But God says in His Word, "There is no need for fear. No need to be downtrodden and discouraged and faint of heart. For I have overcome the world!" He wants us to be strong. After all, we have every reason to be—Christ promises to go with us everywhere we go. Reach out to Him and He will transform your anxious spirit into courage and joy!

I choose to take Your hand right now, Lord, and together
we will do this thing called life! Amen. —A.H.

Big Faith

*Peter said, "I don't have a nickel to my name, but what I do have,
I give you: In the name of Jesus Christ of Nazareth, walk!" He
grabbed him by the right hand and pulled him up. In an instant his
feet and ankles became firm. He jumped to his feet and walked.*
ACTS 3:6–8 MSG

Jesus' disciple Peter didn't always show himself to be a man of great
faith. But in Acts 3 we see that he has grown as a follower of Christ.
In fact, it seems Peter's faith as an apostle has now become quite
powerful and effective.

Our faith can also be powerful and effective. When we ask God
for something, we may not know the exact date or hour when our
request will be answered—whether in that very moment or in the life
to come—but we are invited to ask, and we are expected to believe.
If we do trust the Lord, it is counted as righteousness. It is big faith!

*Lord, please show me how to trust You in all things, and even
when the answer to my prayer doesn't arrive exactly the way
I want it to or in my timing, please help me not to doubt Your
goodness and mercy. Remind me that You are always working
things for good for those who love You. Amen. —A.H.*

Those Ugly Little Barbs

*May the words of my mouth and the meditation of my heart
be pleasing to you, O LORD, my rock and my redeemer.*
PSALM 19:14 NLT

Maybe you were at a church party or gathering at work and somebody—who really grates on your nerves—said something that set you off. No, you didn't take the high road—you had to spit out that little barb. After you saw a flicker of shock on the woman's face, the light dimmed in her eyes. She slinked away amid the awkward stares, and instead of offering an apology, you tried to justify your insult. And so goes the way of human relationships.

But it's not God's way.

Maybe our life-verse should be Psalm 19:14, and we should commit it to memory. That way when we are tempted to release a few sharp arrows, we will remember how a faith-filled follower of Christ should really think and act. Because even if we try hard to hide our thoughts and irritations and judgments, what is in one's heart eventually comes out of one's mouth.

I'm so sorry, Lord, for the way I've acted in the past—for insulting people in more ways than I can count. I don't want to grieve Your Holy Spirit with what's in my heart or with what comes out of my mouth. Help me to be more like You every day! Amen. —A.H.

That Moment of Panic

The LORD says, "I will guide you along the best pathway
for your life. I will advise you and watch over you."
PSALM 32:8 NLT

If you enjoy hiking—then at some point you may experience being
lost. Maybe you're on a trail and decide to head back the way you
came. After a while, you don't recognize anything. Not the trees,
rocks—not anything. You question, "Did I take a wrong turn? Why
is this map so confusing? Did I bring enough water and food?
What will I do when it gets dark?" At some point, after you've tried
everything, you start to scream for help. But no one calls back. You
begin to sweat, but not from the heat.

God is there, and He's waiting for you to look up and call out
to Him.

Life can feel just like that lost, wild-eyed moment in the woods.
You don't know which way to go in your job, marriage, or with your
kids. What if you take a wrong turn? You worry that you could get
disoriented and lose your way. Yes, life throws you into a full-body
panic. But there is hope.

God is there, and He's waiting for you to look up and call out
to Him.

Lord Jesus, I welcome Your divine light on my path.
Please guide me, advise me, and watch over me. Amen. —A.H.

Still Holding On

I know that my redeemer lives, and that in the end he will stand on the earth. And after my skin has been destroyed, yet in my flesh I will see God; I myself will see him with my own eyes—I, and not another. How my heart yearns within me!

JOB 19:25–27

Sometimes we need a model of true faith. Even though Job wasn't a perfect man, he could be called a hero of his life-story. He suffered greatly in many different ways. Basically, he lost it all, but he never chose to curse God and die. Instead he reaffirmed that his Redeemer lives, and that he yearned to see Him with his own eyes one day. In other words, no matter how utterly bleak things looked for Job and no matter how thoughtlessly cruel his friends were to him, he faithfully trusted God.

When we feel as though all is lost, are we still full of the hope that the Bible promises?

Sometimes God's hope is all that's left in the ashes of this world. But the good news is that this hope we have in the Lord is far more than enough—it's everything.

Always choose hope. Job did. And it served him very well indeed.

Lord, I praise You for Your gift of hope. I love You! Amen. —A.H.

Celebrating Life!

Because you are precious to me.
You are honored, and I love you.
ISAIAH 43:4 NLT

If you've ever seen an old, shabby shoe that has been pitched along the side of the road, it's a sight that can be both comical and forlorn. Why the sad part? Maybe it's seeing what was once valuable so easily tossed aside, never to be noticed or appreciated again.

Easy to see where this train of thought could go. Except for those with the mental illness of hoarding, our society tends to chuck things, which is why we have mountains of garbage we don't know what to do with. Unfortunately, when culling out what is seemingly unusable in our lives, sometimes people get lumped in with those old shoes. We can see it in people's eyes when they ignore or fail to show respect to an elderly person. We can sense it in the violent arguments of those who no longer cherish the beauty and life and miracle that grows inside a mom-to-be.

If we say we truly trust God, then we should always love one another as God loves us. May we always celebrate life—no matter how old, no matter how small.

Lord, teach me to cherish all that You cherish!
In Jesus' name I pray. Amen. —A.H.

The Days to Come

She is clothed with strength and dignity;
she can laugh at the days to come.
PROVERBS 31:25

Say you're at a tea party, and one of the ladies mentions that she just lost her job, as well as her home. Then that same woman throws her head back in laughter. *Hmm.* You might not chuckle. You might feel more like edging away from her. Laughing at the future doesn't—from the world's vantage point—seem like a logical or even sane response to all the many things that can go wrong in our lives.

And yet when we read about the much-beloved Proverbs 31 woman, we see that if we trust God with all our hearts, we can feel free to smile and laugh. We don't have to live our lives in "cringe mode," as if ready for the next horrific blow. There will be trouble in this earthly life, as Jesus reminds us, but He has made a promise to never leave us or forsake us.

As Christians, we can trust God with our future—no matter how badly the world continues to fall from grace—no matter the wars or terrors or evil around us. We are in the hands of almighty God, and that is the perfect place to be.

Lord Jesus, I'm ready to be clothed with strength and dignity.
Thank You that I can laugh at the days to come. Amen. —A.H.

Drinking in the Peace

"Peace I leave with you; my peace I give you.
I do not give to you as the world gives. Do not
let your hearts be troubled and do not be afraid."
JOHN 14:27

If there was a specialty blend you could buy at a local coffee shop that would bring peace, people would gather in such mobs that you would never see the end of the line. In fact, the demand would be astronomical.

But there's no true peace without Christ. Only deceptive emotions, illusive harmony, and a temporary absence of war can be derived from this fallen world. But through Christ, we can know the real deal. One way we can drink in His peace is through His living Word, which includes an understanding of God's love for us, the beauty and peace of redemption through Christ, and the knowledge of His second coming!

In the meantime, until the day of Jesus' return—which may be soon—remember this: Do not let your hearts be troubled. The Lord gives you His peace. . . .

I trust You, Lord, with all my heart. Thank You for Your
supernatural peace that surpasses all understanding.
May Your Holy Spirit teach me how to share Your
peace with this needy world. Amen. —A.H.

Go Forth in Faith, in Hope, and in Love!

For this reason I kneel before the Father, from whom every family in heaven and on earth derives its name. I pray that out of his glorious riches he may strengthen you with power through his Spirit in your inner being, so that Christ may dwell in your hearts through faith. And I pray that you, being rooted and established in love, may have power, together with all the Lord's holy people, to grasp how wide and long and high and deep is the love of Christ, and to know this love that surpasses knowledge—that you may be filled to the measure of all the fullness of God.

Ephesians 3:14–19

About the Authors

Bestselling and award-winning author **Anita Higman** has fifty books published. She's been a Barnes & Noble "Author of the Month" for Houston and has a BA in the combined fields of speech communication, psychology, and art. A few of Anita's favorite things are traveling to exotic places, antiquing, fairy-tale everything, gardening (even though she has no idea what's she's doing), all things Jane Austen, making brunch for her friends, and writing with Marian Leslie for the past few years!

Feel free to drop by Anita's website at anitahigman.com or connect with her on her Facebook Reader Page at https://www.facebook.com/AuthorAnitaHigman. She would really enjoy hearing from you!

Marian Leslie is a writer and freelance editor. This is her fourth collaboration with her good writing friend Anita. Though Marian has lived in southwestern Ohio for much of her life, she has ventured far and wide through the pages of many good books. When she's not writing, you can kind find her in thrift shops or used bookstores—always looking for a bargain, especially if it's old and odd.

You Also Might Like . . .

When I'm On My Knees—
20th Anniversary Edition

When I'm on My Knees has blessed more than a million readers since its 1997 release, and now it's available in a beautiful 20th anniversary edition! With themes like praise, forgiveness, healing, trials, love, God's faithfulness, and worship, Anita Corrine Donihue's encouraging devotional thoughts will touch all aspects of your life.

Hardback / 978-1-68322-484-6 / $12.99

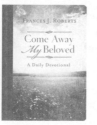

Come Away My Beloved
Daily Devotional

Author Frances J. Roberts started a quiet phenomenon with her book *Come Away My Beloved*, and now excerpts from her beloved writings—including *Come Away, Dialogues with God, Progress of Another Pilgrim*, and *On the Highroad of Surrender*—are available in a beautiful, printed hardcover package. This devotional features the New King James Version of scripture.

Hardback / 978-1-68322-482-2 / $16.99

Trusting Jesus Every Day

This devotional compilation will enhance a woman's spiritual journey as she learns to trust Jesus completely with her whole heart. Dozens of devotions will inspire women of all ages to become just who God created them to be—women of confidence, women of beauty, women of joy, and women of tranquility.

Hardback / 978-1-63058-850-2 / $14.99

New Every Morning Devotional Journal

Here is a delightful women's devotional journal that reminds Christian women of all ages that God is faithful and His mercies are new every morning. Thoughtful readings, lovely prayers, inspiring quotations, and scripture passages speak to the hearts of readers.

Hardback / 978-1-68322-292-7 / $16.99